Tennis's
Most Wanted

Also by Floyd Conner

Baseball's Most Wanted
Football's Most Wanted
Basketball's Most Wanted
Golf's Most Wanted
Wrestling's Most Wanted
Olympics' Most Wanted

Tennis's Most Wanted

The Top 10 Book of Baseline Blunders, Clay Court Wonders, and Lucky Lobs

Floyd Conner

Brassey's, Inc.

WASHINGTON, D.C.

Library of Congress Cataloging-in-Publication Data

Conner, Floyd, 1951–
    Tennis's most wanted : the top 10 book of baseline blunders, clay court wonders, and lucky lobs / Floyd Conner.— 1st ed.
        p.   cm.
Includes bibliographical references and index.
    ISBN 1-57488-363-1
    1. Tennis—Miscellanea. I. Title.

    GV996 .C65 2002
    796.342′02—dc21

                                        2002006642

Printed in Canada.

Brassey's, Inc.
22841 Quicksilver Drive
Dulles, Virginia 20166

Designed by Pen & Palette Unlimited.

First Edition
10 9 8 7 6 5 4 3 2 1

Contents

List of Photographs   x

Introduction   xi

First Serves   1
Notable tennis firsts

Origins   5
How the game evolved

Rules of the Game   9
Rules are meant to be changed

Balls and Rackets   13
Leather balls and spaghetti rackets

Easy Aces   17
The hardest servers in tennis

Strange Shots   21
Unorthodox techniques of champions

The One and Only   25
One-of-a-kind tennis feats

The Sporting Life   31
Tennis players who excelled in other sports

Celebrity Tennis   35
The rich and the famous

Clothes Encounters of the Tennis Kind   39
Tennis fashion plates

Money Shots   43
Underpaid tennis stars

Rocket and the Flying Dutchman   47
Tennis's best nicknames

Super Brat, Nasty, and the Hustler   51
Nicknames they would rather forget

The Name Game   57
The sport's most interesting names

Lefties   61
Outstanding tennis southpaws

Doubles Anyone?   65
Two rackets are better than one

Teen Terrors   69
The youngest men's tournament winners

Teen Phenoms   73
Female tennis sensations

You're Never Too Old   77
Players not slowed by age

Marathon Singles Matches   81
It seemed like they would never end

Marathon Doubles Matches   85
Twice the action

Record Breakers   89
They set marks that still stand

Most Majors Singles Titles: Men   93
Major accomplishments for men

Most Majors Singles Titles: Women   **97**
Career Grand Slam leaders

Most Majors: Men   **101**
Singles, doubles, and mixed doubles titles

Most Majors: Women   **105**
Queens of the court

Most Tournament Victories: Men   **109**
Men's tennis biggest winners

Most Tournament Victories: Women   **113**
Women who win

The Greatest Men Players   **117**
Budge, Borg, and Big Bill

The Greatest Women Players   **121**
King, Court, and Connolly

Tennis's Greatest Feats   **125**
The best of the best

Court Artists   **129**
The game's most stylish players

Forgotten Greats   **133**
Tennis's unsung heroes

The Grand Slam and Beyond   **137**
Top tennis competitions

The Davis Cup   **143**
Memorable moments from the Cup

Going for the Gold   **147**
Olympic tennis

Dual Citizenships   **151**
Players with more than one country

Players Who Never Won a Grand Slam Title   **155**
Major championships eluded them

Players Who Never Won at Wimbledon   **159**
They never raised the trophy at Centre Court

Players Who Never Won the U.S. Open   **163**
They could not win in New York

Players Who Never Won the French Open   **167**
They never triumphed in Paris

Never Number One: Men   **171**
Male stars who never reached the top

Never Number One: Women   **175**
Female players who failed to reach the pinnacle

Embarrassing Losses   **179**
Tennis's most one-sided matches

Classic Collapses   **183**
They let matches slip away

All in the Family   **187**
Famous tennis families

Family Ties   **191**
Tennis's most prominent parents

The Old College Try   **197**
NCAA champions who became top professionals

Love Matches   **201**
Romance on the Court

Battle of the Sexes   **207**
Great matches between men and women

They've Come a Long Way   **213**
Women's struggle for tennis equality

African American Stars   **217**
Black players who made an impact on the sport

Great Rivalries   **223**
Every champion needs a rival

Memorable Matches   **229**
Matches to remember

Ultimate Upsets   **233**
Tennis's most unlikely victors

Spoilers   **237**
They ruined Grand Slam bids

Tennis Believe It or Not   **241**
It really happened

Colorful Characters   **245**
Tennis's most outrageous personalities

Biggest Controversies   **249**
Scandals and controversies

Temper Tantrums   **255**
Players who lost their cool

Fanatics   **261**
Spectators who crossed the line

Early Retirement   **265**
They took an early out

Incredible Injuries   **269**
Illnesses and injuries

Match Points   **273**
Noteworthy tennis lasts

Bibliography   **277**

Index   **279**

About the Author   **289**

List of Photographs

Jimmy Connors   29

John McEnroe   52

Martina Navratilova   92

Steffi Graf   115

Pete Sampras   166

Andre Agassi   203

Serena Williams   219

Bjorn Borg   228

Anna Kournikova   251

Yevgeny Kafelnikov   272

Introduction

Tennis began as the sport of kings. In its early form, tennis could be a dangerous game. Many players were killed when they were struck in the head with the hard leather balls used at the time. King Louis X of France died in 1316 when he caught a chill after drinking an urn of ice-cold water following a strenuous match. Another French king, Charles VIII, suffered a fatal injury after hitting his head on the door frame on his way to the tennis court. At the moment his wife Anne Boleyn was being executed, England's King Henry VIII was enjoying a spirited game of tennis.

The modern game of lawn tennis was invented in Great Britain in the 1870s. The All England Croquet Club set aside a court for tennis. In 1877, the first Wimbledon Championships were played. The first men's winner, Spencer Gore, expressed doubt that the game would ever become popular. Joshua Pim, the Wimbledon champion in 1893 and 1894, played under an assumed name because he was afraid that being known as a tennis player would hurt his medical practice. Since its inauspicious beginnings, tennis has become one of the most popular recreational and spectator sports.

Tennis's Most Wanted pays tribute to the game's most outrageous players. The book contains top-ten lists of the game's most inept players, errant shots, and embarrassing losses. The lists feature the unlikeliest heroes, wildest spectators, and most bizarre nicknames, as well as terrible temper tantrums, strange matches, colorful characters, and the most unusual things ever to happen on a tennis court.

In the game of tennis, anything can happen. Frank Kovacs, a champion in the 1940s, sometimes jumped into the stands to applaud his own shots. Jim Courier, one of the best players of the 1990s, jumped into the Yarra River to celebrate winning the Australian Open. In 1904, Frank Riesley and Sydney Smith decided their semifinal Wimbledon match with a coin toss. Nervous in her first match at Wimbledon in 1957, Brazilian M. H. de Amorin served 17 consecutive double faults.

The comedian W. C. Fields played tennis with his racket in one hand and a martini in the other. Ambidextrous Beverly Baker, a finalist at Wimbledon in 1955, switched the racket from one hand to the other to avoid hitting backhands. Italian tennis star Fausto Gardini was known as the "Vampire" because he liked to chew on tennis balls. Fritz Mercur, a top-ten player in the 1920s, was suspended from tennis for a year for selling a $30,000 insurance policy during a tournament. Bobby Riggs's secret to staying young was to take 415 vitamin pills a day.

Not all tennis attire is conservative. Gussy Moran caused a sensation at Wimbledon in 1949 when she wore lace panties. At the 1961 Wimbledon Championships, Pat Stewart wrote her telephone number on her panties. Dick Savitt beat the heat by wearing a bonnet during a steamy Davis Cup match played in Louisville, Kentucky, in 1951, and Anne White lived up to her name by wearing a formfitting white body suit at Wimbledon in 1985.

John McEnroe, tennis's Super Brat, was not the only player to throw temper tantrums. Ilie Nastase behaved so badly that he was disqualified in a match against McEnroe at the 1979 U.S. Open. Earl Cochell was banned from tournament tennis for life following an outburst at the 1951 U.S. Open. Simone Mathieu once slammed a ball into the stands that nearly struck England's Queen Mary. Goran Ivanisevic had to forfeit a match at the 2000 Samsung Open because he had broken all of his rackets in fits of rage.

This book introduces you to more than six hundred of tennis's most wanted players. Their offenses range from poor play to outlandish behavior. Be on the lookout for these individuals.

First Serves

1. WIMBLEDON

Wimbledon is the most prestigious tennis tournament in the world. Originally, Wimbledon was known as the All England Croquet Club. In 1868, one court was set aside for tennis. Nine years later, the first Wimbledon Tennis Championship was played. Twenty-two men entered the tournament. During the tournament two hundred spectators paid one shilling each to watch the play from a three-row grandstand. Tennis was not yet a popular sport, and no matches were scheduled on July 13 and 14 because they would conflict with a cricket match between Eton and Harrow.

2. SPENCER GORE

The first Wimbledon champion was an Englishman named Spencer Gore. He defeated William Marshall 6–1, 6–2, 6–4 in the championship match. A newcomer to the sport, Gore was not very impressed with the game of tennis. He contended that tennis was monotonous and did not compare in excitement to cricket and other sports. "It is boring and will never catch on," he said. After losing in the championship match at Wimbledon the next year, Gore gave up competitive tennis and returned to rackets, a game similar to squash.

3. MAUD WATSON

The first women's singles competition at Wimbledon occurred in 1884. Thirteen women contested. The winner was Maud Watson, who defeated her sister, Lilian, 6–8, 6–3, 6–3 in the championship match. Watson defended her title successfully in 1885.

4. RICHARD SEARS

Nineteen-year-old Richard Sears was the first U.S. Open champion in 1881. Sears defeated William Glyn 6–0, 6–3, 6–2 in the title match. Sears was so dominant that he won the first seven U.S. Open championships.

5. MAY SUTTON

May Sutton was only 16 years old when she won her first U.S. Open championship in 1904. The next year she became the first American woman to win at Wimbledon.

6. U.S. OPEN SEEDING

Seeding is used in tennis to rank top contenders in a tournament. The purpose of seeding is to keep the best players from playing one another in the early rounds. The first seeding at the U.S. Open took place in 1922. One of the reasons for the seeding was that two of the best women players, Molla Mallory and Suzanne Lenglen, had met in the second round of the 1921 Open. Until 2001 the top 16 players were seeded in most tournaments. A new rule was implemented so that the seedings were expanded to 32. The reason for the change was to reduce the chances that top-seeded players would be ousted in the early rounds by tough unseeded players.

7. **FRED PERRY**

In 1935, Fred Perry won the French Open to become the first player to win all four major championships. The four majors are the Australian Open, French Open, Wimbledon, and the U.S. Open; together they comprise the Grand Slam. The Englishman won eight Grand Slam singles titles between 1933 and 1936.

8. **DON BUDGE**

The first player to win all four Grand Slam tournaments in the same year was American Don Budge. He completed the historic sweep in 1938. Budge turned professional the next year.

9. **MAUREEN CONNOLLY**

The first woman to win the Grand Slam was Maureen Connolly. She swept the four majors in 1953 when she was only 18 years old. The next year she broke her leg in a riding accident and retired from tennis.

10. **PYLE TOUR**

The first professional tennis tour was started by promoter C. C. Pyle in 1926. He signed Suzanne Lenglen, Mary Browne, Vincent Williams, Howard Kinsey, Paul Peret, and Harvey Snodgrass. They toured the United States and played a series of exhibition matches.

Origins

Games similar to tennis were played in ancient Egypt and Greece. Here are some milestones in the development of the game.

1. JEU DE PAUME

An early form of tennis known as jeu de paume originated in France in the twelfth century. Also known as court tennis, jeu de paume was an Olympic event at the 1908 London Olympics.

2. LOUIS X

Tennis has long been a favorite game of royalty. In the early fourteenth century, King Louis X of France played a game known as royal tennis. In 1316, the king caught a chill and died after drinking an urn of ice water following a strenuous game of tennis. The king, who reigned only two years, was 27 years old at the time of his death.

3. BANNED IN BRITAIN

Tennis was also popular in England in medieval times. In fact, it became too popular in the opinion of lawmakers. During the early fifteenth century, statutes were passed that forbade playing tennis because it was felt that men were neglecting their archery practice to play the game.

4. HENRY V

The ban on tennis in England did not last long. Henry V, the English king from 1413 to 1422, took up the game after he received some tennis balls from the French dauphin as a gift.

5. HENRY VIII

Another English king who became a tennis convert was Henry VIII, the monarch from 1509 to 1547. The king had four courts at his palace at Whitehall. Henry rarely lost a match and considered himself the champion of England. It is likely that most of his opponents, fearful of the king's wrath if they defeated him, let Henry win.

6. PETER STUYVESANT

Peter Stuyvesant was a major political figure in New York in the seventeenth century. As governor, he passed some laws that were unpopular with the people. In 1653, a convention of delegates passed a resolution that no new laws be passed without their consent. Stuyvesant, always the diplomat, replied that he derived his authority from God and not from some "ignorant subjects." In 1659, Stuyvesant signed a proclamation that prohibited playing tennis during time set aside for church services. Tennis had become so popular that church attendance had dropped.

7. WILLIAM HICKEY

In 1767, William Hickey formed a tennis club near London. The game was called field tennis, and the club claimed it was their invention.

8. WALTER CLOPTON WINGFIELD

The modern game of tennis derived from lawn tennis. The game was patented by Walter Clopton Wingfield in 1874. The next year Wingfield published the rules for his game of lawn tennis. The rules have evolved over the years, but today's sport is basically the game he created.

9. MARY OUTERBRIDGE

Shortly after Walter Wingfield patented lawn tennis, the game was brought to the United States. The person generally given credit for introducing modern tennis to America was Mary Outerbridge. She first played the game in Bermuda and returned to the United States with a net, two rackets, and some tennis balls. In 1874,

Outerbridge convinced her brother to build a tennis court at the Staten Island Cricket and Baseball Club where he was a manager.

10. **JAMES DWIGHT**

Another person who deserves credit for bringing the game of lawn tennis to America was James Dwight. Often called "The Father of American Tennis," Dwight built a court in Nahant, a seaside resort ten miles outside of Boston. In 1876, the first tennis tournament in the United States was held there.

Rules of the Game

The rules of tennis have changed over the years.

1. THE SERVE

In today's game, the player stands behind the baseline to serve to the opponent. The player must hit the ball over the net so that it lands in the opponent's service area. Five hundred years ago tennis was played in courtyards. The server was required to hit the ball off a sloping roof. The ball deflected off the roof and onto the returner's side of the court.

2. HANS REDL

To serve, a player tosses the ball into the air and strikes it with the racket. A variation of the rule was made in 1947 to accommodate Austrian player Hans Redl, who lost an arm during World War II. The rule was expanded to allow a disabled player to use the racket to toss the ball into the air prior to the serve.

3. **FOOT FAULT**

A foot fault is called on a player who steps on or over the baseline during the serve. Originally, a foot fault was called when a player's feet left the ground during the serve. Today's players leap into the air and generate power on the serve.

4. **THE HOURGLASS SHAPED COURT**

Tennis courts have not always been rectangular in shape. The original court devised by Walter Clopton Wingfield was shaped like an hourglass. It was narrow at the net and wider at the baseline.

5. **THE NET**

The regulation net is three feet high at the center and three feet, six inches high at the side posts. Prior to 1892, the net could be as high as five feet at the post, making it almost impossible to hit a passing shot down the line. At the other extreme, a two-foot-high net was used for a brief time in the nineteenth century.

6. **THE OVERSIZED RACKET**

Prior to 1976, there were no specific rules regulating the size and shape of tennis rackets. Until that time rackets could be any shape, size, or weight, and could be made of any material. It was necessary to regulate rackets when oversized rackets were introduced in the late 1970s.

7. **YELLOW TENNIS BALLS**

Traditionally, tennis balls were white. In the 1970s, World Championship Tennis (WCT) began using yellow tennis balls. In 1986, Wimbledon instituted the use of yellow balls because they were easier to see on television.

8. **TWO BOUNCES**

A player is permitted one bounce on his side of the court before the ball must be returned. During the nineteenth century, women were allowed two bounces because they wore long skirts and were not able to move as quickly across the court.

9. **POINTS**

Under the current scoring system a player must win at least four points to win a game. Since a player must win by at least two points, it is often necessary to win more than four points to win the game. Since a player must win a game by at least two points, additional points are often required. In the early days of tennis, a player had to win at least 15 points to win a game.

10. **THE TIEBREAKER**

Prior to the introduction of the tiebreaker, players were required to win a set by at least two points. As a result, sets could often become marathon affairs. In the mid-1960s, the tiebreaker was introduced at the Prentice Cup. The original tiebreaker was created by Jimmy

Van Alen. A nine-point sudden-death tiebreaker was used at the 1970 United States Professional Indoor Championships in Philadelphia. The 12-point tiebreaker made its first appearance at Wimbledon in 1971.

Balls and Rackets

As the rules of tennis have evolved, so has the equipment.

1. LEATHER BALLS

Tennis balls have not always been the fluffy ones we play with today. During medieval times, tennis balls were often made of leather with a core of wound human hair. The balls were so hard that many players were killed after being struck in the head.

2. ANTONIO SCAINO

The first tennis book was written by Antonio Scaino and published in Venice in 1555. According to Scaino, rackets, then known as battoirs, were shaped to suit the feelings of the individual players. They came in various shapes and sizes.

3. WALTER CLOPTON WINGFIELD

Walter Clopton Wingfield is the man credited with inventing lawn tennis. In the 1870s he sold tennis sets that included four rackets, a set of balls, and a net. The set cost five guineas.

4. J. M. HEATHCOTE

When lawn tennis began to become popular, the balls were rubber coated. In 1874, J. M. Heathcote suggested that the balls be covered with white flannel. The flannel-covered balls bounced better and were easier to control.

5. MAUD WATSON

Maud Watson won the first Wimbledon women's singles title in 1884. She used a homemade oblong-shaped racket.

6. F. W. DONNISTHORPE

The first oversized racket was used by F. W. Donnisthorpe in the early 1920s. He made his own racket that he used at Wimbledon. The Donnisthorpe racket was loosely strung and had a larger-than-average-sized head.

7. GIORGIO DE STEFANI

Italian Giorgio de Stefani was ambidextrous. During the match he would shift his racket from hand to hand so that he was always hitting forehands. He wanted to use two rackets, one for each hand. In 1931, a rule was implemented to ban the use of a player using two rackets at once.

8. **THE SPAGHETTI RACKET**

A new racket was used by Australian Barry Phillips-Moore at the French Open in 1977. The spaghetti racket, as it was called, had plastic tubing that resembled spaghetti. The strings had much less tension than the conventional racket and caused exaggerated top spin, which was difficult for the opponent to gauge. During the years, players using the controversial racket pulled off a number of upsets. It was determined that the racket double-hit the ball, and it was banned.

9. **JIMMY CONNORS**

Jimmy Connors was the first major tournament player to abandon the traditional wooden racket for a larger metal one. In the late 1970s, Connors began using the Wilson 2000 aluminum model. Other players soon realized the advantages of using a racket with a larger sweet spot and began using the metal rackets.

10. **JOHN McENROE**

As metal rackets became the norm with tournament players, manufacturers introduced lighter-weight materials. John McEnroe was the last major tournament player to change from a wooden to a metal racket. In 1983, John McEnroe became the first player to win Wimbledon using a graphite racket.

Easy Aces

Boris Becker was nicknamed "Boom Boom" because of his booming serve. The fastest serves can reach speeds approaching 150 miles per hour. Players who were known for their powerful serves include Pancho Gonzales, Jack Kramer, Colin Dibley, and Dick Savitt. This group includes some of the hardest servers in tennis history.

1. BILL TILDEN

Bill Tilden was one of the most talented players to ever play the game. He had the reputation of being the fastest server of his day. In 1931, his serve was measured at an incredible 163 miles per hour. Although speed-measuring machines may not have been as accurate as they are today, certainly Tilden was one of the hardest servers in tennis history.

2. **MICHAEL SANGSTER**

Englishman Michael Sangster had one of the hardest serves in tennis. In June 1963, Sangster's serve was measured at 154 miles per hour.

3. **ROSCOE TANNER**

Roscoe Tanner, a left-hander from Lookout Mountain, Tennessee, once had a serve measured at 153 miles per hour. Tanner used his blazing serve to help him win the 1977 Australian Open, and he was a finalist at Wimbledon in 1979. What made his serve even more impressive was that he used a wooden racket for most of his career.

4. **GREG RUSEDSKI**

Another left-hander with a rocket serve was Greg Rusedski. A top-ten player in the late 1990s, Rusedski hit a 148-miles-per-hour serve, the fastest ever recorded on the ATP (Association of Tennis Professionals) Tour.

5. **GORAN IVANISEVIC**

One of the best servers in tennis today is Croatian Goran Ivanisevic. Despite serving 37 aces in the 1992 Wimbledon finals, he lost the match to Andre Agassi. During 1996, Ivanisevic served more than 1,500 aces. He set a Wimbledon record by serving 213 aces and won his first men's singles title in 2001.

6. ELLSWORTH VINES

Ellsworth Vines had a legendary serve. At match point of the 1932 Wimbledon championship match against Bunny Austin, Vines unleashed a mighty ace. The serve was so fast that Austin claimed he could not tell if it went by on his forehand or backhand side.

7. ANDY RODDICK

One of the game's biggest hitters among the young stars is American Andy Roddick. On May 30, 2001, the 18 year old served 37 aces in a second-round match against Michael Chang at the French Open. The 37 aces were the most ever recorded on the slow clay surface in Paris. Roddick won the match 5–7, 6–3, 6–4, 6–7, 7–5.

8. KEVIN CURREN

For years Kevin Curren was one of the most feared servers in tennis. His serve took him all the way to the finals of the 1985 Wimbledon Championship. He lost to another big server, Boris Becker, 6–3, 6–7, 7–6, 6–4.

9. ROBERT FALKENBURG

Many experts consider American Robert Falkenburg one of the hardest servers ever to play the game. Falkenburg defeated John Bromwich 7–5, 0–6, 6–2, 3–6, 7–5 in the finals of the 1948 Wimbledon Championship.

10. **LEW HOAD**

Lew Hoad used his powerful serve to win back-to-back Wimbledon singles titles in 1956 and 1957. The big Australian dominated men's tennis in 1956, winning three of the four Grand Slam titles and competing as a finalist at the U.S. Open.

Strange Shots

N ot every tennis technique is textbook.

1. **BEVERLY BAKER**

Beverly Baker was a finalist in the women's singles at Wimbledon in 1955. Ambidextrous, she switched her racket back and forth between hands in order not to have to hit backhand shots.

2. **CHARLOTTE DOD**

Charlotte Dod was 15 years old when she won her first Wimbledon title in 1887. Dod won five Wimbledon singles titles and was never defeated there. What made the achievement even more remarkable was that she served underhanded.

3. **ELLEN HANSELL**

Ellen Hansell won the U.S. Open in 1887, the first year women were allowed to compete. Hansell used a squared-off racket and served sidearm. She completely depended on her groundstrokes and never went to the net.

4. MICHAEL CHANG

In the fourth round of the 1989 French Open, Michael Chang developed a cramp during a match against Ivan Lendl. The cramp became so bad that Chang had to serve underhanded. Despite the cramp, Chang rallied from two sets down to defeat Lendl in a match that lasted 4 hours and 37 minutes. Chang went on to win the title.

5. JANA NOVOTNA

Jana Novotna and Helena Sukova met Gigi Fernandez and Mary Joe Fernandez in the 1996 Wimbledon doubles finals. Novotna pulled a stomach muscle and had to serve underhanded. Fernandez and Fernandez won the match 7–6, 6–4.

6. ELLSWORTH VINES

Ellsworth Vines was one of the most powerful players of the 1930s. The winner of both Wimbledon and the U.S. Open men's singles titles in 1932, Vines had a peculiar windmill motion on his groundstrokes. He would wind up and uncoil before striking the ball.

7. HERBIE FLAM

Herbie Flam was a finalist in the men's singles at the 1950 U.S. Open. Flam had many technical weaknesses in his game. His serve was abysmal, and his forehand can best be described as herky-jerky. Flam overcame his deficiencies with his amazing court coverage skills and highly competitive nature.

8. BEPPINO MERLO

Beppino Merlo was an outstanding Italian player in the 1950s. Merlo had a very unorthodox grip. He was one of the first players to use a two-handed backhand. He placed his right hand halfway up the handle like a baseball player choking up on the bat.

9. MRS. A. TYRWHITT-DRAKE

Mrs. A. Tyrwhitt-Drake competed at Wimbledon in the 1880s. The Englishwoman gripped her racket far up the handle. Although the unorthodox technique limited her power and compromised her ability to reach shots, she was one of the best players of her time.

10. BETTINA BUNGE

Bettina Bunge was a top-ten player in the early 1980s despite less-than-perfect technique. She rarely transferred her weight while swinging the racket and did not even turn sideways when hitting the ball at the net. The unorthodox technique did not stop Bunge from winning more than a half-dozen tournaments.

The One and Only

Frank Hadow, a tea planter from Ceylon, won the men's singles title at the 1878 Wimbledon Championships. Hadow commented that he saw little future in the game of tennis and returned to Ceylon, becoming the only Wimbledon champion to give up tennis to return to planting tea. Here are some more one-of-a-kind tennis facts.

1. MOLLA MALLORY

Suzanne Lenglen only lost one singles match between 1919 and 1926. In the second round of the 1921 U.S. Open, Lenglen was trailing 37-year-old Molla Mallory 6–2, 2–0 when, in tears, she informed the umpire she was too ill to continue. Whether Lenglen was really ill or disheartened by her uncharacteristically poor play remains a mystery.

2. **FRANK SHIELDS**

American Frank Shields was the only player ever to forfeit a Wimbledon final to nurse an injury. In the 1931 Wimbledon men's finals, Shields was scheduled to meet Sidney Wood for the championship. However, Shields had injured his ankle in a previous match and decided to forfeit the match against Wood in order to rest his ankle for an upcoming Davis Cup match against Great Britain.

3. **ILIE NASTASE and ARTHUR ASHE**

The match between Ilie Nastase and Arthur Ashe at a tournament in Stockholm was a contrast in temperaments. Nastase, the volatile Romanian, was notorious for his court tantrums. By contrast, Arthur Ashe always seemed to be in control. Throughout the match, Nastase stalled, argued calls, and infuriated officials with his antics. Ashe was leading 1–6, 7–5, 4–1 when he decided he'd had enough of Nastase's outbursts. Ashe walked off the court, and officials were forced to disqualify him. Tired of Nastase's behavior, they also disqualified him; it was the only time both players were disqualified in a match. The next day, the officials reversed their ruling and awarded the match to Ashe. Since it was a round robin tournament, both Ashe and Nastase were allowed to play their remaining matches. In fact, Nastase defeated Bjorn Borg in the championship match.

4. **TOM OKKER**

Tom Okker of the Netherlands is the only player to receive first-prize money at the U.S. Open without winning the tournament. In the championship match of the 1968 U.S. Open, Okker lost to Arthur Ashe 14–12, 5–7, 6–3, 3–6, 6–3. Since Ashe was still an amateur and could not receive prize money, Okker was awarded the $14,000 first-prize check.

5. **JOHN HARTLEY**

John Hartley was the only minister to win the men's singles title at Wimbledon. He won the championship in 1879 and 1880. Between matches, Reverend Hartley preached to his congregation in Yorkshire.

6. **ROD LAVER**

The only player to win the Grand Slam twice was Rod Laver. "Rocket" Rod won the Slam as an amateur in 1962. He then turned professional and was prohibited from competing in Grand Slam tournaments for the next five years. In 1969 Laver became the only player to win the Grand Slam twice.

7. **BOBBY RIGGS**

The only player to win the singles, doubles, and mixed doubles titles in his only appearance at Wimbledon was Bobby Riggs. He achieved the unique triple at the 1939 Wimbledon championships. Wimbledon was not held from 1940 to 1945 due to World War II. By the time the tournament resumed play in 1946, Riggs had turned professional and was ineligible to compete.

8. JIMMY CONNORS

Jimmy Connors was the only player to win the U.S. Open on three different surfaces. In 1974, Connors defeated Ken Rosewall when the championship was played on grass. Two years later, he defeated Bjorn Borg in four sets on clay. In 1978, Connors outlasted Borg in a five-setter on the new hard court surface at the National Tennis Center. Connors also won on the hard court surface at Flushing Meadows in 1982 and 1983.

9. KATHY HORVATH

Martina Navratilova was practically unbeatable in 1983. She won 83 of 84 matches. Her only loss occurred in the fourth round of the French Open. She was defeated by Kathy Horvath 6–4, 0–6, 6–3.

10. KATHLEEN MCKANE

The only player to defeat Helen Wills in singles competition at Wimbledon was Kathleen McKane. She defeated Wills 4–6, 6–4, 6–4 in the 1924 women's final. Wills never lost another singles match at Wimbledon. Between 1927 and 1938, she was ladies' champion at Wimbledon eight times.

In 1978, Jimmy Connors became the only player to have won the prestigious U.S. Open on three different surfaces—grass, clay, and hard court.

The Sporting Life

These tennis stars were accomplished in other sports.

1. ALTHEA GIBSON

Althea Gibson was one of the best athletes ever to play tennis. She won the women's singles titles at Wimbledon and at the U.S. Open in both 1957 and 1958. After retiring from competitive tennis, Gibson played golf on the LPGA (Ladies Professional Golf Association) Tour from 1964 to 1969.

2. CHARLOTTE DOD

Charlotte Dod won her first Wimbledon singles title in 1887 at the age of 15. Dod won her fifth Wimbledon title in 1893. Virtually unchallenged, Dod retired from tennis to concentrate on other sports. In 1904 she won the British Women's Golf Championship. At the 1908 London Olympics, Dod was a silver medalist in archery. Dod was also an outstanding rower and hockey player.

3. ELLSWORTH VINES

Ellsworth Vines won both Wimbledon and the U.S. Open in 1932. In the 1940s, Vines became one of the top professional golfers in the United States. Vines won the 1945 Southern California Pro Golf Open.

4. JAROSLAV DROBNY

Jaroslav Drobny holds the distinction of being the only athlete to win an Olympic medal in ice hockey and a men's singles title at Wimbledon. Drobny won a silver medal as a member of the Czechoslovakian hockey team at the 1948 St. Moritz Winter Olympics. Drobny defeated Ken Rosewall 13–11, 4–6, 6–2, 9–7 to win the 1954 Wimbledon men's singles title.

5. TONY TRABERT

Tony Trabert averaged nearly seven points a game as a member of the 1951 University of Cincinnati basketball team. That same year he was the NCAA (National Collegiate Athletic Association) tennis champion. Between 1953 and 1955, Trabert won five Grand Slam singles titles. In 1955 he won the men's singles championships at the French Open, Wimbledon, and the U.S. Open.

6. MAX WOOSNAM

Englishman Max Woosnam teamed with countryman Oswald Turnbull to win the men's doubles gold medal at the 1920 Antwerp Olympics. Woosnam was captain of the British Davis Cup team. He also captained the Cambridge University cricket team and the English football team.

7. KEN MCGREGOR

Ken McGregor was the 1952 Australian Open men's singles champion. Although McGregor was talented in singles, he really excelled in doubles. McGregor and partner Frank Sedgman won the Grand Slam in doubles in 1951. McGregor was also an outstanding Australian rules football player.

8. MARTY RIESSEN

Illinois native Marty Riessen played basketball at Northwestern University. A good basketball player, he was even better at tennis. Riessen won the French Open men's doubles title with partner Arthur Ashe in 1971. Riessen and Tom Okker were one of the most successful doubles teams of the 1970s. In 1976 they won the men's doubles championship at the U.S. Open.

9. IVAN LENDL

Ivan Lendl won 94 singles titles during his illustrious tennis career. An avid golfer, Lendl frequently plays in celebrity tournaments. He hopes to be able to compete on the Senior Golf Tour when he turns 50 in the year 2010.

10. Ion TIRIAC

Ion Tiriac had his greatest success in tennis as a player when he teamed with doubles partner Ilie Nastase. The rugged Tiriac also played hockey on the Romanian national team.

Celebrity Tennis

In the 1930s British tennis champion Fred Perry was friends with many Hollywood stars, including Marlene Dietrich, Errol Flynn, Douglas Fairbanks, Mary Pickford, and David Niven. Here are some more examples of the Hollywood-tennis connection.

1. CATHY LEE CROSBY

In 1964, Cathy Lee Crosby played at Wimbledon. She lost in the first round to Jacqueline Rees-Lewis of France 6–3, 6–1. She also played doubles with her sister, Linda, as her partner. Crosby was more successful in her acting career. She played the role of Wonder Woman in a 1974 made-for-television movie and was a regular on the hit series *That's Incredible!*, which aired from 1980 to 1984.

2. BROOKE SHIELDS

Brooke Shields's grandfather, Frank Shields, was a finalist in men's singles at the U.S. Open in 1930 and at Wimbledon in 1931. She was married to tennis superstar

Andre Agassi from 1997 to 1999. Shields has starred in numerous films, including *Pretty Baby* and *Blue Lagoon,* as well as the television series *Suddenly Susan.*

3. RICKY NELSON

Fifteen-year-old Ricky Nelson reached the finals of the 1955 Oregon State Boys' Championship. Nelson was defeated by Bruce Campbell 6–2, 6–2. Nelson gained fame as the youngest son in the long-running sitcom, *The Adventures of Ozzie and Harriet.* He also appeared as a gunfighter in the cult movie classic, *Rio Bravo,* which starred John Wayne and Dean Martin. One of the first teen idols, Nelson recorded thirty-five Top 40 hits between 1957 and 1972. Two of his hits, "Poor Little Fool" and "Travelin' Man," reached number one. Ricky Nelson was inducted into the Rock and Roll Hall of Fame in 1987.

4. VINCE VAN PATTEN

Vince Van Patten is the son of actor Dick Van Patten. For a time in the 1980s, Van Patten pursued careers in acting and as a professional tennis player. Van Patten starred in films such as *Hell Night* and *Charley and the Angel.* On the pro tennis tour Van Patten defeated many of the top players.

5. VIJAY AMRITAJ

Vijay Amritaj was the greatest tennis player from India. Between 1973 and 1986, he won 16 tournaments on the ATP tour. In 1983, Amritaj played an Indian agent in the James Bond film *Octopussy.*

6. **CLARK GABLE**

Clark Gable won an Academy Award in 1934 for his performance in *It Happened One Night,* but he is best remembered for his portrayal of Rhett Butler in *Gone With The Wind.* A remark he made had a major impact on women's tennis in the late 1930s. Gable attended the Pacific Southwest Championship with his wife, Carole Lombard. They came to see Alice Marble, a top tennis player whom they knew. Gable leaned over and said to Lombard, "We all like Alice. She's a nice person, but she doesn't have it." At the time it was thought that Marble lacked the killer instinct. Marble overheard the remark and, motivated, won the match in just 20 minutes. A tremendous serve-and-volley player, Marble won three consecutive U.S. Opens from 1938 to 1940 and was Wimbledon women's champion in 1939.

7. **W. C. FIELDS**

W. C. Fields made some of the funniest films of the 1930s and 1940s, including *The Fatal Glass of Beer, You Can't Cheat an Honest Man,* and *Never Give A Sucker an Even Break.* Fields was known for his love of a good drink, and that carried over onto the tennis court. Fields played with a martini in one hand and a racket in the other. Worried about spilling a drink, Fields refused to chase after balls, but he was effective at returning shots within his reach.

8. **WILLIAM RANDOLPH HEARST**

William Randolph Hearst owned a newspaper publishing empire in the early decades of the twentieth century. The millionaire built an incredible 130-room mansion in California that he called San Simeon. Hollywood's biggest stars were frequent guests at San Simeon. Hearst enjoyed playing doubles tennis matches with his guests. However, he did not like to run, and his unfortunate partner had to chase after all the balls out of Hearst's reach.

9. BILL TILDEN

Bill Tilden was not only the greatest male tennis player of the 1920s, he also knew many of the rich and famous of his day. In New York, he lived in a suite at the Algonquin Hotel and was friends with authors F. Scott Fitzgerald and Ernest Hemingway. Tilden had ambitions to be a writer and produced plays on Broadway. During the 1930s, Tilden's career as a tennis player was nearing an end, so he moved to Hollywood in hopes of becoming an actor. Although his acting career never took off, he did give tennis lessons to numerous Hollywood stars. Some of Tilden's pupils included Charlie Chaplin, Douglas Fairbanks, and Joseph Cotten.

10. ELEANOR TENNANT

One of the best tennis coaches of all time was Eleanor "Teach" Tennant. Bobby Riggs and Maureen Connolly were just two of the many champions she coached. She was also known as "Hollywood's Coach" because of the number of stars she instructed. Clark Gable and Carole Lombard were two of Tennant's celebrity clients.

Clothes Encounters of the Tennis Kind

For years white was the only accepted color for tennis attire. These players helped expand the boundaries of tennis fashion.

1. GUSSY MORAN

Although the sight of a woman's panties might not cause a stir today, it created a sensation in 1949. Staid old Wimbledon was not ready for the surprise American Gussy Moran had in store for them. "Gorgeous Gussy" wore a short dress and lace-trimmed panties designed by Ted Tinling. When word got out about Gussy's lace panties, photographers lined the court. Some photographers even lay on the ground to get a better shot of the panties. The panties controversy was subject for debate in the British Parliament, and there was concern that the royal family might be offended. Moran did not win the tournament, but she certainly received the most attention.

2. **PAT STEWART**

Another panties controversy occurred at Wimbledon in 1961. American Pat Stewart, in an apparent attempt to improve her social life, had her telephone number embroidered on her panties.

3. **KAROL FAGEROS**

American Karol Fageros was the Anna Kournikova of her day—as famous for her good looks as for her tennis. Ted Tinling, the man who designed Gussy Moran's lace panties, made special gold lamé panties for Fageros for the 1958 Wimbledon championships. Officials were not amused and banned the panties.

4. **RENÉ LACOSTE**

Frenchman René Lacoste won three French Opens, two Wimbledons, and two U.S. Opens between 1925 and 1929. Always fashion conscious, Lacoste coveted an alligator skin bag he saw in a shop window. His coach promised to buy it for him if he won the tournament. Lacoste lost in the final, but the impression of the alligator bag stayed with him. Once he retired from tennis, Lacoste founded his own sportswear company, and he used a crocodile as his logo.

5. **ROSEMARY CASALS**

Rosemary Casals was famous for her colorful tennis outfits. In 1972, Casals was forced to change her dress because officials believed that the purple design on the outfit formed the letters V. S., an advertisement for the Virginia Slims women's tour. One of Casals's most memorable outfits was a stars and stripes dress designed by Ted Tinling.

6. SUZANNE LENGLEN

It was said that Suzanne Lenglen never wore the same color outfit in two successive matches. Lenglen had many of her tennis outfits designed by noted French couturier Jean Patou. While most women players of the time were wearing petticoats and corsets on the court, Lenglen wore calf-length silk dresses that were considered brazen. Lenglen was particularly fond of bright colors such as red and orange, and her white stockings were twisted at the top and held up by French coins. She wore a fur coat to courtside even on the hottest days.

7. ANNE WHITE

Anne White lived up to her name during a 1985 match against Pam Shriver at Wimbledon. She dressed in a formfitting white bodysuit. White and Shriver split the first two sets before darkness halted play. Although the suit covered more of her body than a conventional tennis dress, Wimbledon officials considered it indecent and forced White to change the following day. Shriver won the match in three sets.

8. JOY GANNON

Designer Ted Tinling struck again at Wimbledon in 1948. British player Joy Gannon was barred from the competition for wearing a Tinling frock because it had bits of color on it, a violation of the all-white rule.

9. DICK SAVITT

During a 1951 Davis Cup match against Japan in Louisville, Kentucky, Australian Dick Savitt found a way to beat the heat. Savitt wore a white bonnet to shield his eyes from the bright sun.

10. VENUS WILLIAMS

In the first round of the 2001 Australian Open, Venus Williams turned heads with an outfit that displayed some cleavage. "I loved the outfit," she said. For the next round, the outfit was stitched up to reveal less skin. Williams is studying to be a fashion designer once her tennis career is over

Money Shots

By the time she was 20 years old, Venus Williams had signed endorsement deals valued at a reported 70 million dollars. Pete Sampras has earned more than 40 million dollars in prize money during his career. Tennis players have not always been so highly paid.

1. BJORN BORG

At the 1978 Italian Open, Bjorn Borg faced local favorite Adriano Panatta. Italian fans tried to break Borg's concentration by throwing coins at the stoic Swede, but Borg simply picked up the coins and pocketed them. He further irritated fans by defeating Panatta in five sets.

2. JULIE HELDMAN

On September 23, 1970, nine women professional tennis players signed one-dollar contracts to start their own tennis tour. The new tour was started in response to the inequality of purse money between men and women. The symbolic signing was held at the Houston, Texas, home of Gladys Heldman. The nine players who attended the ceremony were Billie Jean King, Rosemary Casals, Nancy Richey, Peaches Bartkowicz, Gladys Heldman's daughter Julie, Kerry Melville, Val Ziegenfuss, Judy Dalton, and Kristy Pigeon. The women's tour was a success, and women's purses soon were on a par with men's.

3. KITTY GODFREE

Until the late 1960s Wimbledon was a competition limited to amateur players. Kitty Godfree, the 1924 Wimbledon champion, received a prize voucher worth five guineas from the jeweler Mappin and Webb for her victory. Godfree recalled years later that she had to accumulate several prize vouchers before she was able to turn them in for a gift she wanted.

4. MAUD WATSON

Maud Watson was the first women's champion at Wimbledon in 1884. She was presented with a silver flower basket worth 20 guineas. The runner-up received a hand mirror and silver brush valued at 10 guineas.

5. MARTINA NAVRATILOVA

Martina Navratilova earned more than 20 million dollars during her tennis career. At the beginning of her career, Navratilova was given $17 a day by the Czech Tennis Federation, which kept the rest of her prize money. Understandably, Navratilova defected to the United States in 1975.

6. IVAN LENDL

Tennis professionals donated their rackets to be sold at a Lake Tahoe auction to benefit the United Cerebral Palsy Research and Education Foundation. A racket used by Evonne Goolagang sold for $2,750 and a Vitas Gerulaitas racket was auctioned for $2,250. The top price of $3,000 was bid on a racket that belonged to John McEnroe. For some reason, a racket owned by three-time U.S. Open champion Ivan Lendl brought only $200. The auction raised half a million dollars for the charity.

7. BILLIE JEAN KING

In 1973, Billie Jean King earned $100,000 for her Battle of the Sexes exhibition match against Bobby Riggs. By contrast King received only $7,500 for her Wimbledon victory that year.

8. MARGARET SMITH COURT

Margaret Smith Court became the second woman to win the Grand Slam. Her combined earnings in 1970 for winning the French Open, Wimbledon, the U.S. Open, and Australian Open were just $15,000.

9. **VIRGINIA WADE**

Virginia Wade defeated Billie Jean King 6–4, 6–2 in the women's championship match at the 1968 U.S. Open. The 1968 Open was the first in which professionals were permitted to play. Wade collected $6,000 for her victory.

10. **JOHN McENROE**

John McEnroe proved that money isn't everything. In the 1980s he turned down a million dollars to play an exhibition match in South Africa because he disagreed with the South African government's policy of apartheid.

Rocket and the Flying Dutchman

Tim Wilkison was nicknamed "Dr. Dirt." The doubles team of Harold Solomon and Eddie Dibbs was known as the "Bagel Twins." Here are more of tennis's most memorable nicknames.

1. THE LEANING TOWER OF PASADENA

Stan Smith won the U.S. Open singles title in 1971 and was the 1972 Wimbledon champion. The 6′3″ Californian leaned into his serve and was nicknamed the "Leaning Tower of Pasadena."

2. THE BARCELONA BUMBLEBEE

Arantxa Sanchez Vicario won the French Open in 1989, 1994, and 1998 and was the U.S. Open champion in 1994. The Spanish player is known for her remarkable court coverage, thereby earning the nickname the "Barcelona Bumblebee."

3. **THE FOUR MUSKETEERS**

Henri Cochet, René Lacoste, Jean Borotra, and Jacques Brugnon dominated men's tennis in the 1920s. The Frenchmen won 19 major championships between 1924 and 1932 and held the Davis Cup from 1927 to 1933. The men were so linked that they were called the "Four Musketeers."

4. **ROCKET**

Rod Laver was arguably the greatest tennis player who ever lived. He is the only player to win the Grand Slam twice. Laver was given the nickname "Rocket" by famed coach Harry Hopman. The name perfectly described Laver's powerful strokes.

5. **THE FLYING DUTCHMAN**

Tom Okker was the most successful Dutch player in tennis history. Okker won more than one hundred singles and doubles titles in the 1960s and 1970s. One of the fastest players of his day, Okker was known as the "Flying Dutchman."

6. **THE GODDESS**

Marguerite Broquedis was tennis's first pinup. The French beauty won the French Open in 1913 and 1914. She was considered so attractive that she was referred to as the "Goddess."

7. RABBIT

Wendy Turnbull was a singles finalist in three major championships between 1977 and 1980. The Australian really excelled in doubles competition, however, winning nine Grand Slam doubles titles. Turnbull was so quick around the court that she was nicknamed "Rabbit."

8. THE BIG CAT

Miroslav Mecir won eight tournaments during the 1980s, and the highlight of his career was a gold medal in the men's singles at the 1988 Olympics. The 6'3" Czech had a huge stride, and his long reach allowed him to get to balls that were out of the reach of most players. His catlike quickness earned him the nickname the "Big Cat."

9. THE LITTLE WONDER

Charlotte Dod won her first Wimbledon women's singles title in 1887 at the age of 15. By 1893, Dod had won five Wimbledons. The tiny Dod was called the "Little Wonder." Despite her lack of size, Dod was such a good athlete that she won the British Women's Golf Championship in 1904 and a silver medal in archery at the 1908 London Olympics.

10. MISS CHOP AND DROP

Elizabeth Ryan won more than 650 tournaments between 1912 and 1934. One of the best doubles players in history, she won 12 women's doubles crowns and seven mixed doubles titles at Wimbledon. She was known as "Miss Chop and Drop" because she chopped her forehand and had an excellent drop shot.

Super Brat, Nasty, and the Hustler

N ot every nickname is complimentary.

1. SUPER BRAT

If anyone ever lived up to a nickname, it was John McEnroe. He won 77 singles titles, including four Wimbledon championships, but McEnroe will always be remembered for his outbursts during matches. Most of his venom was directed at unfortunate linesmen when he believed they blew a call. The frequent tantrums earned McEnroe the nickname of "Super Brat."

2. NASTY

Ilie Nastase was an incredibly gifted tennis player who was often his own worst enemy. Nastase won the 1972 U.S. Open and probably would have won many more major tournaments had it not been for his lapses of concentration. Nastase often clowned to amuse the spectators. When he wasn't mugging for the fans,

"Super Brat" John McEnroe shows a bit of his famous emotion on the court. McEnroe's outbursts, usually directed at linesmen and referees, earned him fines, suspensions, and a rare disqualification in the 1990 Australian Open for abusive language.

Nastase was usually throwing a fit. His bad behavior earned him the nickname of "Nasty."

3. **THE GHOST**

Willoughby James Hamilton won the men's singles title at Wimbledon in 1890. The Irishman was so pale and thin that he was referred to as the "Ghost."

4. **MUSCLES**

Ken Rosewall was not the most imposing looking tennis player. The 5'7" Australian defeated more powerful rivals with finesse and speed. Rosewall won eight Grand Slam singles titles during his heyday from the early 1950s to the mid-1970s. The ease with which Rosewall played was summed up by his philosophy of "getting the maximum results with a minimum of effort." Rosewall was called "Muscles" because it seemed like he did not have any.

5. **LITTLE MISS ALMOST**

An outstanding junior player, Sarah Palfrey never won Wimbledon and was 28 years old before she became a champion at the U.S. Open in 1941. Before she finally won at Forest Hills, Palfrey had finished as runner-up twice at the U.S. Open. Because of her near misses, she was given the unwanted nickname "Little Miss Almost."

6. **LITTLE MISS GRUNT**

Monica Seles dominated women's tennis in the early 1990s. During one stretch, she won eight of nine possible

Grand Slam tournaments. Every time she hit a shot, Seles let out with a highly audible grunt. The habit resulted in her being called "Little Miss Grunt."

7. LITTLE MISS POKER FACE

Helen Wills Moody's last name was the antithesis of her court demeanor. She was known as "Little Miss Poker Face" because she was expressionless during her matches. Like a good poker player, she never let her opponent know what she was thinking. Between 1923 and 1938, she won 19 Grand Slam singles titles.

8. THE ICE MAIDEN

In many ways, Chris Evert was the modern version of Helen Wills Moody. Her icy manner on the court disguised a highly competitive nature. The "Ice Maiden" racked up one 158 tournament victories during her illustrious career.

9. THE HUSTLER

Bobby Riggs won Wimbledon and the U.S. Open in 1939. After his retirement from competitive tennis, Riggs supplemented his income by making wagers with wealthy acquaintances. Usually, Riggs would agree to a match in which he would play with a preposterous handicap. Two of his favorite ploys were to play while carrying a suitcase or with a dog on a leash.

10. **THE VAMPIRE**

Italian Fausto Gardini was one of the top players of the 1950s. One of the fiercest competitors in tennis history, he had the odd habit of biting tennis balls. Gardini was nicknamed the "Vampire."

The Name Game

These players had tennis's most memorable names. Meet Birdie, Bitsy, Bunny, and Brownie.

1. MARGARET SMITH COURT

Margaret Smith Court not only had the perfect tennis name, she also had the ideal game. Court dominated women's tennis in the 1960s and early 1970s. Her 24 Grand Slam singles titles are the most won by any player.

2. PEANUT LOUIE

Peanut Louie may sound like the name of a vendor at the ballpark, but, in fact, she was a top tennis player in the 1980s. In 1985, she was ranked in the top 20.

3. PEACHES BARTKOWICZ

Peaches Bartkowicz was the number-eight-ranked women's player in 1969. She is best remembered as one of the nine women who broke ranks with the established tour and began their own in 1970.

4. ANNA SMASHNOVA

An overhand smash in tennis usually results in a win for the player. Possessing one of tennis's best names, Anna Smashnova won the 1999 Tashkent Open.

5. BITSY GRANT

Bryan Grant was nicknamed the "Mighty Atom" because of his small size. The 5′4″, 120-pound Grant was better known as "Bitsy." While Grant may have been small in size, there was nothing small about his talent. He won the National Clay Court titles in 1930, 1934, and 1935, and is a member of the Tennis Hall of Fame.

6. BUNNY AUSTIN

Bunny Austin was the first male tournament player to wear shorts. The Englishman wore shorts at the 1932 Wimbledon championship. He reached the finals but lost to Ellsworth Vines 6–4, 6–2, 6–0. Six years later, Austin finished runner-up at Wimbledon to American Don Budge.

7. BUDGE PATTY

Edward "Budge" Patty was born in Arkansas, but he became one of the most sophisticated tennis players. In 1950, Patty won the men's singles at both Wimbledon and the French Open. The elegant player moved to Paris and, when he was not winning tennis tournaments, liked to paint.

8. BIRDIE TOWNSEND

Bertha "Birdie" Townsend was one of the United States' first women tennis champions. She helped organize one of the first tournaments for women, the Philadelphia Championship, in 1886. At age 19, Townsend won her first U.S. Open title in 1888 and repeated as champion the next year.

9. BROWNIE BROWN

Mary "Brownie" Brown was an outstanding player in the early twentieth century. The Californian won three consecutive U.S. Open titles from 1912 to 1914.

10. BOUNDING BETTY NUTHALL

British star Betty Nuthall was known for her ability to cover the court. "Bounding Betty" won the women's singles title at the 1930 U.S. Open.

Lefties

Maureen Connolly was a natural left-handed player in the 1940s, but she changed to right-handed play as a youth because it was thought that left-handers could not be champions. Since then, many left-handed players have become tennis stars. Some left-handers who became champions include Monica Seles, Neale Fraser, Guillermo Vilas, Guy Forget, Goran Ivanisevic, Petr Korda, Henri Leconte, and Thomas Muster.

1. ROD LAVER

Rod Laver was the first tennis player to earn a million dollars in career prize money. The only player to win the Grand Slam twice, Laver forever ended the notion that left-handed tennis players were somehow inferior to righties.

2. MARTINA NAVRATILOVA

Martina Navratilova proved that a left-hander could also dominate women's tennis. The powerful Navratilova won nine Wimbledon singles crowns with her serve-and-volley game.

3. JIMMY CONNORS

Between 1972 and 1989, Jimmy Connors won 109 tournaments. The ultimate competitor, Connors won five U.S. Open singles titles.

4. JOHN McENROE

Jimmy Connors's great rival in the early 1980s was fellow American and left-hander John McEnroe. McEnroe was even more combative than Connors and just as accomplished a player. McEnroe played many of the greatest matches in tennis history.

5. ANN JONES

Ann Jones was the first left-handed woman to win the Wimbledon singles title. The British woman defeated Billie Jean King 3–6, 6–3, 6–2 in the 1969 women's championship match.

6. JAROSLAV DROBNY

Czech lefty Jaroslav Drobny won the French Open men's singles titles in 1951 and 1952. In 1954, he defeated Ken Rosewall in the men's final at Wimbledon.

7. TONY ROCHE

Australian Tony Roche was the 1966 French Open champion. A fine singles player who was a finalist at both Wimbledon and the U.S. Open, Roche excelled at doubles. He teamed with fellow Aussie John Newcombe to win 11 Grand Slam doubles titles, including five at Wimbledon.

8. **ART LARSEN**

In 1950, American Art Larsen became the first left-hander to win the men's singles championship at the U.S. Open. Larsen defeated Herbie Flam 6–3, 4–6, 5–7, 6–4, 6–3 in the final match.

9. **MANUEL ORANTES**

Manuel Orantes of Spain was one of the best male tennis players of the 1970s. Orantes won 32 tournaments during his career and was the 1975 U.S. Open champion.

10. **ANDRES GOMEZ**

The best tennis player that Ecuador has ever produced, Andres Gomez won 21 tournaments. The highlight of his career came in 1990 when he upset Andre Agassi to win the French Open singles title.

Doubles Anyone?

Some players are better at doubles than at singles. The team of Mark Woodforde and Todd Woodridge won five consecutive Wimbledon doubles championships from 1993 to 1997. Doubles specialist Gigi Fernandez teamed with Mary Joe Fernandez (no relation) to win the gold medals in women's doubles in 1992 and 1996. Australian Ken Fletcher teamed with Margaret Smith Court to win the mixed doubles Grand Slam in 1963.

1. TOM OKKER

Tom Okker's court speed helped make him one of the best doubles players in tennis history. His 78 doubles titles are an all-time record.

2. PETER FLEMING

Peter Fleming was John McEnroe's favorite doubles partner. Tall and powerful, Fleming was an ideal complement to McEnroe's finesse and agility. Together, they won 57 doubles titles and seven Grand Slam championships.

3. ROSEMARY CASALS

Barely five feet tall, Rosemary Casals's lack of size kept her from being a top-ranked singles player. Nevertheless, her speed and incredible arsenal of shots made her one of the best doubles players of the late 1960s and early 1970s. Casals teamed with Billie Jean King to win five Wimbledon doubles titles between 1967 and 1973. Casals also won four United States Open doubles championships.

4. BRIAN GOTTFRIED

Brian Gottfried won 25 singles titles but was even more successful in doubles. He won 54 doubles championships during the 1970s and 1980s. Thirty-nine of his doubles titles came with partner Raul Ramirez. Among the championships Gottfried and Ramirez won were Wimbledon and the French Open.

5. JOHN BROMWICH and ADRIAN QUIST

The doubles team of John Bromwich and Adrian Quist were unbeatable in the Australian Open between 1938 and 1950. Bromwich and Quist won the men's doubles competition in 1938, 1939, and 1940. The tournament was not held from 1941 to 1945, due to World War II. After the tournament resumed in 1946, the Aussie duo won five consecutive doubles titles, giving them a streak of eight in a row.

6. **ANDERS JARRYD**

Anders Jarryd was one of the many excellent young Swedish players to follow Bjorn Borg. During the 1980s, Jarryd was one of the most successful doubles players in the world. He won 47 doubles titles with 15 different partners. Jarryd won the U.S. and French Opens three times each.

7. **THELMA COYNE LONG**

Australian Thelma Coyne Long won her national singles titles in 1952 and 1954. She dominated the women's doubles at the Australian Open, winning 12 times. Ten times she teamed with Nancy Wynne Bolton, and twice she won with Mary Hawton.

8. **DARLENE HARD**

Darlene Hard won the women's singles at the U.S. Open in 1960 and 1961. As good as she was in singles, she was twice as good in doubles. Hard won five consecutive U.S. Open women's doubles titles between 1958 and 1962. During that period she had three different partners. Hard added a sixth U.S. Open doubles championship in 1969. She won Wimbledon four times with three different partners (Maria Bueno, Althea Gibson, and Jeanne Arth). Hard also won the French Open women's doubles title three times.

9. NATASHA ZVEREVA

Natasha Zvereva was an outstanding doubles player in the 1990s. The Russian won 18 Grand Slam doubles titles. Zvereva won six French Opens, five Wimbledons, four U.S. Opens, and three Australian Opens.

10. KEN McGREGOR

Ken McGregor of Australia teamed with Frank Sedgman to win the men's doubles Grand Slam in 1951. The next year, McGregor won the Australian Open, French Open, and Wimbledon men's doubles titles.

Teen Terrors

These talented male players were already champions while still in their teens.

1. VINCENT RICHARDS

Vincent Richards was only 15 when he teamed with Bill Tilden to win the men's doubles title at the 1918 U.S. Open. Richards won a total of five U.S. Open doubles championships between 1918 and 1926.

2. AARON KRICKSTEIN

The youngest man to win an ATP singles championship was Aaron Krickstein. He was 16 years and 2 months old when he won the Tel Aviv Open in 1983.

3. BORIS BECKER

Boris Becker was only 17 when he won his first Wimbledon singles championship in 1985. Becker also won at Wimbledon in 1986 and 1989, and was runner-up there four times between 1988 and 1995.

4. **MICHAEL CHANG**

In 1987, 15-year-old Michael Chang became the youngest man ever to win a match in the main draw of the U.S. Open. Two years later, Chang became the youngest man to win the French Open singles title.

5. **MATS WILANDER**

Although Mats Wilander never quite achieved the fame and success of his fellow countryman Bjorn Borg, he did win seven Grand Slam singles titles during his career. At age 17, Wilander won the French Open in 1982. Wilander won three Grand Slam championships in 1988.

6. **ANDRE AGASSI**

Another teen sensation was Andre Agassi. He was 17 when he won his first singles title at Itaparica, Brazil, in 1987.

7. **JIMMY ARIAS**

American Jimmy Arias was 18 in 1982 when he won his first tournament in Tokyo. Arias had a respectable career but never lived up to the promise of his youth.

8. **PETE SAMPRAS**

A player who did live up to the high expectations was Pete Sampras. He was 18 when he won his first professional singles title at Philadelphia in 1990. Later that year, Sampras won his first Grand Slam championship at the U.S. Open.

9. **ANDY RODDICK**

The young player touted to be the next great American champion is Andy Roddick. He was 18 when he won his first singles title in a tournament in Atlanta in 2001.

10. **LLEYTON HEWITT**

Lleyton Hewitt was only 16 when he competed in his first Australian Open. In 2001, Hewitt became the youngest male player to be ranked number one.

Teen Phenoms

E ver since 15-year-old Charlotte Dod won her first Wimbledon singles title in 1887, many teenage girls have become tennis champions. Steffi Graf was 13 when she first competed in Grand Slam tournaments.

1. TRACY AUSTIN

Tracy Austin was 14 when she won her first Avon Futures tournament in Portland, Oregon, in 1977. At the 1979 U.S. Open, Austin defeated Chris Evert 6–4, 6–3 for her first Grand Slam title. She was 16 years and 8 months old, making her the youngest U.S. Open champion in history.

2. KATHY RINALDI

In 1981, 14-year-old Kathy Rinaldi became the youngest player to win a match at Wimbledon. Rinaldi had a solid career but never achieved the success expected of her.

3. MARY JOE FERNANDEZ

Fourteen-year-old Mary Joe Fernandez was the youngest player to win a singles match at the U.S. Open. Fernandez's first win at the U.S. Open occurred in 1985. Although Fernandez never won the U.S. Open, she was a top women's player for more than a decade.

4. ANDREA JAEGER

Andrea Jaeger was only 15 when she joined the women's tour in 1980. At the 1981 French Open, the 15 year old teamed with 16-year-old Jimmy Arias to become the youngest mixed doubles champions in the tournament's history. A top-five-ranked player by age 16, Jaeger never won a Grand Slam singles title, although she was a finalist at Wimbledon in 1983.

5. MARTINA HINGIS

One of the greatest prodigies in tennis history was Martina Hingis. In March 1997, the 16 year old became the youngest women's player to be ranked number one in the world. That year, she became the youngest player of the modern era to win a Grand Slam singles title when she won the Australian Open. Before the year was finished, Hingis had won her first Wimbledon and U.S. Open singles championships.

6. MAUREEN CONNOLLY

Few players have achieved as much success in a short career as Maureen Connolly. Connolly was 16 when she won her first U.S. Open singles title. She was only 18 in 1953 when she became the first woman to win the Grand Slam. In one of tennis's greatest tragedies, Connolly was severely injured in a horse riding accident in 1954 and was only 19 when her competitive career ended.

7. **MONICA SELES**

Monica Seles was only 16 when she defeated Steffi Graf 7–6, 6–4 to win the 1990 French Open. The teenager dominated women's tennis in the early 1990s, winning eight Grand Slam singles crowns before her career was derailed by a senseless stabbing by a spectator at a tournament in Hamburg in 1993. Seles has won just one Grand Slam title, the 1996 Australian Open, since the attack.

8. **PAM SHRIVER**

Pam Shriver was only two months past her sixteenth birthday when she reached the finals of the 1978 U.S. Open. She lost to Chris Evert 7–6, 6–4 and never reached another Grand Slam singles final.

9. **JENNIFER CAPRIATI**

Jennifer Capriati became the first 14 year old to be ranked in the top ten. Within a year she had reached the semifinals at the U.S. Open, Wimbledon, and the French Open. In 1992, the 16 year old defeated Steffi Graf to win the gold medal in tennis at the Barcelona

Summer Olympics. Personal problems kept her out of tennis for three years. In 2001, Capriati achieved one of the greatest comebacks in tennis history by winning the Australian and French Opens.

10. NATASHA CHYMREVA

Natasha Chymreva was actually disqualified for being too young. The teenager won her first match of The Championships at Roehampton, England, in 1974. It was discovered that she was 15, one year below the 16-year-old age limit. Chymreva was forced to withdraw from the tournament.

You're Never Too Old

Tournament tennis is usually dominated by players in their teens and twenties. Occasionally players can maintain their competitive edge well past their physical prime. Pancho Gonzales played outstanding tennis well into his forties. The players in this section achieved major success at ages when most players are slowing down or retiring.

1. JEAN BOROTRA

Known as the "Bounding Basque" Jean Borotra won the men's singles at Wimbledon in 1924 and 1926. The ageless Frenchman continued to compete at Wimbledon until 1964 when the 65 year old played in the men's and mixed doubles events.

2. ARTHUR GORE

Life began at forty for Englishman Arthur Gore. He was 41 in 1909 when he won his third Wimbledon singles title, and he was a finalist at Wimbledon at age 44 in 1912. Gore was 59 when he competed at Wimbledon for the last time in 1927.

3. FRANK PARKER

American Frank Parker won the French Open in 1948 and 1949. In 1965, 36 years after his first appearance, the 52-year-old Parker played in the U.S. Open. He lost in the first round to Arthur Ashe.

4. BLANCHE BINGLEY

Blanche Bingley was 36 when she won her sixth Wimbledon singles title in 1900. In 1912, the 48 year old was still good enough to reach the semifinals at Wimbledon.

5. MARGARET OSBORNE DU PONT

Margaret Osborne du Pont was 29 when she won her only Wimbledon singles title in 1947. At age 44, she teamed with Neale Fraser to win the mixed doubles championship at Wimbledon.

6. KEN ROSEWALL

Ken Rosewall was only 18 years old in 1953 when he won his first Australian and French Opens. Incredibly, Rosewall got better with age. At 39, Rosewall was a finalist at both Wimbledon and the U.S. Open. In 1975, at the age of 40, he was ranked number two, his highest world ranking.

7. **GARDNAR MULLOY**

Gardnar Mulloy was 42 when he teamed with Budge Patty to win the 1957 Wimbledon men's doubles championship. Mulloy and Patty outlasted 22-year-old Lew Hoad and 23-year-old Neale Fraser 8–10, 6–4, 6–4, 6–4 in the championship match.

8. **MOLLA MALLORY**

Molla Mallory was 31 when she won her first U.S. Open singles title in 1915. She won her record eighth and final Open title in 1926 at the age of 42.

9. **JIMMY CONNORS**

Jimmy Connors won five U.S. Open singles championships, but his greatest moment at the Open came in a year he did not win. Connors appeared to be over the hill in 1990 when, hampered by an elbow injury, he did not win a match all year. At the 1991 U.S. Open, the 39-year-old Connors made one last run at the title. After a series of exciting comeback victories, Connors lost in the semifinals to Jim Courier.

10. **BILL LARNED**

Bill Larned was 28 when he won his first U.S. Open singles title in 1901. Ten years later he won his seventh U.S. Open championship in 1911.

Marathon Singles Matches

Before the tiebreaker was instituted, matches could go on indefinitely. Here are some of the longest singles matches in tennis history.

1. JOHN BROWN

In the third round of the 1968 Heart of America Tournament in Kansas City, John Brown and Bill Brown played a set that lasted 70 games. John Brown won the first set 36–34 and the second set 6–1.

2. VIC SEIXAS

At the 1966 Philadelphia Grass Championships, 42-year-old Vic Seixas defeated 22-year-old Bill Bowrey in a match that lasted nearly four hours. Seixas lost the first set 32–34 before rallying in the final two sets 6–4 and 10–8.

3. ROGER TAYLOR

The match between Roger Taylor and Wieslaw Gasiorek at the Kings Cup in Warsaw, Poland, in 1966 had not one, but two marathon sets. Taylor dropped the first set 27–29. The second set was even longer, with Taylor prevailing 31–29. The exhausted players concluded their epic match with Taylor winning the final set 6–4.

4. PANCHO GONZALES

The first-round match between Pancho Gonzales and Charlie Pasarell in 1969 was the longest in Wimbledon history. The 41-year-old Gonzales defeated Pasarell, 16 years his junior, 22–24, 1–6, 16–14, 6–3, 11–9. The match was so long that it was played over two days.

5. ROD LAVER

One of the most competitive matches in Australian Open history occurred in the semifinals of the 1969 championships. Rod Laver bested Tony Roche 7–5, 22–20, 9–11, 1–6, 6–3 in a match that lasted 4 hours and 35 minutes.

6. F. D. ROBBINS

American F. D. Robbins defeated Dick Dell in the first round of the 1969 U.S. Open. One hundred games were played during the five-set match. Robbins won the marathon match with scores of 22–20, 9–7, 6–8, 8–10, 6–4.

7. **JAROSLAV DROBNY and BUDGE PATTY**

Spectators who witnessed the championship match at the 1955 Lyons Covered Courts Invitational in Lyons, France, must have thought the match would never end. In a way, it never did. The match featured Jaroslav Drobny, the 1954 Wimbledon champion versus Budge Patty, the 1950 Wimbledon winner. Drobny won the first set 21−19, and Patty took the second 10−8. The third and final set was tied 21−21 when Drobny and Patty agreed to a draw.

8. **JOHN McENROE**

The longest Davis Cup match in history took place in St. Louis, Missouri, in 1982. John McEnroe of the United States was matched against 17-year-old Swedish phenom Mats Wilander. McEnroe outlasted Wilander 9−7, 6−2, 15−17, 3−6, 8−6 in a match that lasted 6 hours and 22 minutes.

9. **LOUISE BROUGH**

American Louise Brough played one 117 games in one day at Wimbledon in 1949. She won the women's singles title with a 10−8, 1−6, 10−8 victory over Margaret du Pont. Brough then teamed with du Pont to defeat Gussy Moran and Pat Todd 8−6, 7−5 in the women's doubles championship. Brough and partner John Bromwich lost in the finals of the mixed doubles.

10. **ELLSWORTH VINES**

Ellsworth Vines came from two sets down to defeat fellow American Chris Sutter 4–6, 8–10, 12–10, 10–8, 6–1 in the men's semifinals at Wimbledon in 1932. Vines easily defeated Bunny Austin in the championship match.

Marathon Doubles Matches

These doubles teams worked overtime to win their matches.

1. DICK DELL and DICK LEACH

A second-round doubles match at the 1967 Newport Casino Invitational in Rhode Island lasted 6 hours and 10 minutes. The team of Dick Dell and Dick Leach defeated Len Schloss and Tom Mozur 3–6, 49–47, 22–20.

2. TED SCHROEDER and BOB FALKENBURG

The men's doubles finals at the 1949 Southern California Championship lasted one 134 games. Ted Schroeder and Bob Falkenburg won the classic five-set match over Pancho Gonzales and Hugh Stewart with scores of 36–34, 2–6, 4–6, 6–4, 19–17.

3. NANCY RICHEY and CAROLE GRAEBNER

Usually matches played on grass are fast-paced, but the women's doubles semifinals at the 1964 Eastern

Grass Championships in South Orange, New Jersey, was an exception. Nancy Richey and Carol Graebner defeated Justina Bricka and Carol Hanks 31–33, 6–1, 6–4.

4. PANCHO SEGURA and ALEX OLMEDO

The team of Pancho Segura of Ecuador and Alex Olmedo of Peru defeated the South African team of Abe Segal and Gordon Forbes 32–30, 5–7, 6–4, 6–4 in the second round of the 1966 Wimbledon championships.

5. MARK COX and ROBERT WILSON

The men's doubles match between the British team of Mark Cox and Robert Wilson and the Americans Charlie Pasarell and Ron Holmburg at the 1967 U.S. Indoor Championships had three epic sets. Cox and Wilson defeated Pasarell and Holmburg 26–24, 17–19, 30–28 in the 6-hour-and-23-minute match.

6. MARGARET DU PONT and BILL TALBERT

The 1948 United States mixed doubles semifinals featured a first set that lasted 52 games. Margaret du Pont and Bill Talbert defeated Gussy Moran and Bob Falkenburg 27–25, 5–7, 6–1. Perhaps worn out by the lengthy semifinal match, Talbert and du Pont lost in the finals to Tom Brown and Louise Brough.

7. NIKKI PILIC and GENE SCOTT

In the first round of the 1966 Wimbledon men's doubles, Nikki Pilic and Gene Scott defeated Cliff Richey and Torben Ulrich 19–21, 12–10, 6–4, 4–6, 9–7.

8. **SARAH PALFREY COOKE and HELEN JACOBS**

The women's doubles semifinal at the 1936 U.S. Open matched Sarah Palfrey Cooke and Helen Jacobs against Alice Marble and Kay Stammers. Cooke and Jacobs defeated Marble and Stammers 21–19, 6–2, but they lost the championship match to Marjorie Van Ryn and Carolin Babcock.

9. **BILL TALBERT and GARDNAR MULLOY**

Bill Talbert and Gardnar Mulloy defeated Don McNeill and Frank Guernsey 3–6, 6–4, 2–6, 6–3, 20–18 in the men's doubles championship match at the 1946 U.S. Open.

10. **JAN GUNNARSON and MICHAEL MORTENSEN**

The tiebreaker was instituted to shorten matches, but the fourth set of a 1985 Wimbledon men's doubles match featured a lengthy final game. Jan Gunnarson of Sweden and his partner Michael Mortensen of Denmark defeated Paraguay's Victor Pecci and Australian John Frawley 6–3, 6–4, 3–6, 7–6. Gunnarson and Mortensen won the fourth-set tiebreaker 26–24.

Record Breakers

These tennis records have stood the test of time.

1. CHERRY CREEK HIGH SCHOOL

The boys' tennis team at Cherry Creek High School in Wheat Ridge, Colorado, did not lose a match for 27 years. The streak lasted from 1972 to 1999. Cherry Creek finally lost a match to Wheat Ridge High School 5–2.

2. HOWARD KINSEY and HELEN MOODY

On February 7, 1936, Howard Kinsey and Helen Moody decided to see how many times they could volley without a miss. Kinsey and Moody rallied for 1 hour and 18 minutes without a miss. They hit the ball across the net 2,001 times. The rally ended when Moody had to leave to give a tennis lesson.

3. VICKY NELSON

Vicky Nelson defeated Jean Hepner 6–4, 7–6 in a match that took place on September 25, 1984, in Richmond, Virginia. Incredibly, the two-set match lasted 6 hours and 31 minutes. One rally lasted 643 strokes, a record for a competitive match. The record rally took 30 minutes to complete. The second-set tiebreaker alone took 1 hour and 47 minutes to complete.

4. ELIZABETH RYAN

Elizabeth Ryan had an amazing year in 1924. She won 75 titles that included 27 singles, 27 doubles, and 21 mixed doubles championships. During her career, Ryan won more than 650 tennis tournaments.

5. CHRIS EVERT

Chris Evert was practically unbeatable on clay. In fact, she did not lose a match on clay from August 1973 to May 1979, a streak of 125 matches. The record-breaking streak ended on May 12, 1979, when Evert lost to Tracy Austin 6–4, 2–6, 7–6 in the semifinals of the Italian Open.

6. PAM SHRIVER and MARTINA NAVRATILOVA

The record for consecutive victories by a doubles team belongs to Pam Shriver and Martina Navratilova. Between April 1983 and July 1985, they won 109 consecutive doubles matches. The streak was broken by

Kathy Jordan and Elizabeth Smylie in the 1985 women's doubles finals at Wimbledon.

7. MARTINA NAVRATILOVA

Martina Navratilova also holds the record for the longest winning streak by a woman player. She won 74 matches in a row before losing to Helena Sukova in the semifinals of the 1984 Australian Open. The winning streak lasted nearly a year.

8. MARGARET SMITH COURT

Margaret Smith Court holds the modern record for tournaments won in a year. Court won 17 singles titles in 1971.

9. LOUISE BROUGH and MARGARET OSBORNE DU PONT

The team of Louise Brough and Margaret Osborne du Pont holds the record for the most women's doubles titles at the U.S. Open. They won 12 doubles titles between 1942 and 1957. Brough and du Pont also combined for five Wimbledon doubles crowns.

10. JIMMY CONNORS

Jimmy Connors has the record for the most tournament victories by a male tennis player. Connors won 109 titles during his career. His final singles title came at the Tel Aviv Open in 1989.

Martina Navratilova stretches to return a volley. Navratilova holds the records for consecutive doubles victories, with Pam Shriver, and the longest winning streak by a woman, a 74-match streak lasting nearly a year.

Most Majors Singles Titles: Men

The four major tennis tournaments are Wimbledon, the U.S. Open, French Open, and Australian Open. A player who is able to win one major is considered a champion. All of the following men won at least seven singles titles.

1. PETE SAMPRAS

When Pete Sampras won his seventh Wimbledon singles title in 2000, he passed Roy Emerson to become the all-time men's Grand Slam singles title leader. Sampras has won 13 Grand Slam singles titles, including four U.S. Opens and two Australian Opens. So far only the French Open title has eluded him.

2. ROY EMERSON

Roy Emerson dominated men's tennis during the early 1960s. The Australian won 12 major singles titles between 1960 and 1967. Half of those Grand Slam victories came at the Australian Open. Emerson won five consecutive Australian Opens from 1963 to 1967. He won the U.S. Open, French Open, and Wimbledon twice each.

3. **BJORN BORG**

Although Bjorn Borg never won the men's singles title at the U.S. or Australian Opens, he still managed to win 11 Grand Slam singles championships. The Swede won six French Opens and five consecutive Wimbledon championships between 1976 and 1980.

4. **ROD LAVER**

Rod Laver won the Grand Slam in both 1962 and 1969. The "Rocket" won four Wimbledon championships and 11 Grand Slam singles titles. Undoubtedly the total would have been higher had Laver not been excluded from playing in the Grand Slam tournaments for five of his prime years because he was a professional.

5. **BILL TILDEN**

Bill Tilden won 10 Grand Slam titles even though he never won the French Open and never played in the Australian Open. "Big Bill" won three Wimbledons and seven U.S. Opens between 1920 and 1930. From 1920 to 1925, Tilden won six consecutive U.S. Open titles.

6. **FRED PERRY**

Englishman Fred Perry won eight Grand Slam titles between 1933 and 1936. Perry won Wimbledon and the U.S. Open three times each and the French and Australian Opens once.

7. IVAN LENDL

Ivan Lendl is remembered for never winning Wimbledon, but the Czech star did win eight Grand Slam singles titles. Lendl won three U.S. Opens, three French Opens, and two Australian Opens.

8. JIMMY CONNORS

Jimmy Connors won eight Grand Slam singles titles. Connors won twice at Wimbledon and once at the Australian Open, but it was at the U.S. Open that Connors really shined. He won five U.S. Open titles between 1974 and 1983.

9. KEN ROSEWALL

Perhaps no tennis player maintained a high level of play for as long as Ken Rosewall. He won his first Grand Slam singles title in 1953 and his last in 1972. Rosewall's eight Slam titles included four Australian, two French, and two U.S. Opens.

10. WILLIE RENSHAW

One of the nineteenth century's greatest players, Willie Renshaw won seven Wimbledon singles titles between 1881 and 1889.

Most Majors Singles Titles: Women

Each of the following women won at least eight Grand Slam titles.

1. MARGARET SMITH COURT

Margaret Smith Court holds the record for the most Grand Slam singles titles with 24. She won the Grand Slam in 1970. Eleven times she was the Australian Open women's singles champion. Court won the French and U.S. Opens five times each and was victorious at Wimbledon on three occasions.

2. STEFFI GRAF

Steffi Graf won the Grand Slam in 1988. Graf won 22 Grand Slam singles titles. Graf won seven Wimbledon, six French Open, five U.S. Open, and four Australian Open titles.

3. HELEN WILLS MOODY

Helen Wills Moody won more Grand Slam singles titles than any other American woman player. Moody won eight Wimbledon, seven U.S. Open, and four French Open titles.

4. CHRIS EVERT

Despite playing in an era with other great women champions such as Martina Navratilova, Billie Jean King, and Evonne Goolagong, Chris Evert won 18 Grand Slam singles titles. A brilliant player on clay, Evert won seven French Opens. She showed her versatility by winning six U.S. Opens, three Wimbledons, and two Australian Opens.

5. MARTINA NAVRATILOVA

Martina Navratilova won 18 Grand Slam singles titles, half of them at Wimbledon. She also won four U.S. Opens, three Australian Opens, and two French Opens.

6. SUZANNE LENGLEN

Suzanne Lenglen won a dozen Grand Slam singles titles despite never winning a U.S. Open or Australian Open title. Unbeatable in the early 1920s, she won six Wimbledon and six French Open singles titles.

7. BILLIE JEAN KING

Billie Jean King won 12 Grand Slam singles titles during her illustrious career. King won six Wimbledon and four U.S. Open titles. She also won the Australian Open in 1968 and the French Open in 1972.

8. MONICA SELES

During the early 1990s, Monica Seles won eight of nine Grand Slam singles titles. Despite being stabbed by a fan in 1993, Seles has won an impressive nine Slam singles titles. She won four Australian Opens, three French Opens, and two U.S. Opens.

9. MAUREEN CONNOLLY

A serious leg injury ended Maureen Connolly's tennis career at age 19. Before her accident, Connolly won the Grand Slam in 1953. Connolly won nine Grand Slam titles while still in her teens. She won three Wimbledons, three U.S. Opens, two French Opens, and one Australian Open.

10. MOLLA MALLORY

Molla Mallory won eight Grand Slam singles titles, all at the U.S. Open. Mallory won her first U.S. Open in 1915 and her final one in 1926.

Most Majors:
Men

There are three competitions at Grand Slam tournaments: singles, doubles, and mixed doubles. Each of these players won at least 18 major championships.

1. ROY EMERSON

Between 1959 and 1971, Roy Emerson won 28 Grand Slam titles. Emerson won 12 singles and 16 doubles competitions. Nine of his victories came at the Australian Open.

2. JOHN NEWCOMBE

John Newcombe is all-time second among men's tennis players in total Grand Slam titles. The Australian won 25 titles between 1965 and 1976. Newcombe won seven singles, 17 doubles, and one mixed doubles championship.

3. FRANK SEDGMAN

Frank Sedgman won 22 major titles; five singles, nine doubles, and eight mixed doubles. What makes his achievement so remarkable is that he won all his major championships in a four-year period from 1949 to 1952. In 1953, Sedgman turned professional and was unable to compete in the Grand Slam events.

4. BILL TILDEN

Bill Tilden won 10 singles, six doubles, and five mixed doubles at the major championships between 1919 and 1932. Sixteen of the 21 titles came at the U.S. Open.

5. ROD LAVER

Rod Laver won 20 Grand Slam titles between 1959 and 1971. Laver won 11 singles, six doubles, and three mixed doubles titles. The total would have been much higher had he not spent many years as a professional.

6. JOHN BROMWICH

Although John Bromwich won only two Grand Slam singles titles, he won 19 major titles from 1938 to 1950. An outstanding doubles player, Bromwich won 13 Grand Slam doubles and four mixed doubles.

7. NEALE FRASER

Neale Fraser was one of the outstanding young Australian players who came to prominence in the

1950s. Fraser's 1960 Wimbledon championship was one of his three Grand Slam singles titles. He also won 11 men's doubles and four mixed doubles between 1957 and 1962.

8. FRED STOLLE

Another Australian who had 18 Grand Slam titles to his credit was Fred Stolle. He won his only Grand Slam singles titles at the 1965 French Open and 1968 U.S. Open. Stolle won 10 men's doubles and six mixed doubles between 1962 and 1969. He formed outstanding doubles teams with Bob Hewitt and Roy Emerson.

9. JEAN BOROTRA

One of the famed French Four Musketeers, Jean Borotra won four singles, nine men's doubles, and five mixed doubles in Grand Slam tournaments from 1925 to 1936. Eight of his 18 major titles came at the French Open.

10. KEN ROSEWALL

Ken Rosewall was equally accomplished as a singles and doubles player. Rosewall won eight singles, nine doubles, and one mixed doubles Grand Slam titles from 1953 to 1972.

Most Majors: Women

The success of women champions in the Grand Slam tournaments has been remarkable. Seven women have won more titles than Roy Emerson, the men's career leader.

1. MARGARET SMITH COURT

The Grand Slam success of Margaret Smith Court may never be duplicated. From 1960 to 1975, she won 62 Grand Slam titles. Court won 24 singles, 19 doubles, and 19 mixed doubles titles.

2. MARTINA NAVRATILOVA

Martina Navratilova won nine of her 18 Grand Slam singles titles at Wimbledon. Navratilova won a record 31 Slam doubles titles and added six mixed doubles crowns. Her total of 55 Grand Slam championships ranks behind only Margaret Smith Court. Navratilova still competes in doubles and mixed doubles so it is conceivable she could add to her total.

3. BILLIE JEAN KING

Billie Jean King won a dozen Grand Slam singles titles and 27 women's and mixed doubles titles. She won a record 20 championships at Wimbledon.

4. MARGARET DU PONT

One of the most underrated women champions was Margaret du Pont. Between 1941 and 1960, she won six singles, 21 doubles, and 10 mixed doubles Grand Slam titles.

5. DORIS HART

Over an eight-year period from 1948 to 1955, Doris Hart won an incredible 35 Grand Slam titles. Hart's greatest success came in doubles. She won 14 doubles and 15 mixed doubles titles.

6. LOUISE BROUGH

Like Doris Hart, Louise Brough won six singles and 35 total Grand Slam titles. From 1948 to 1950, Brough won eight of the nine possible titles at Wimbledon, including all three singles.

7. HELEN WILLS MOODY

Helen Wills Moody won 19 Grand Slam singles titles between 1923 and 1938. She also won nine women's doubles and three mixed doubles titles. Twelve of her victories came at Wimbledon, and she won 11 U.S. Open titles.

8. **ELIZABETH RYAN**

Elizabeth Ryan never won a Grand Slam singles title but she did win 26 Slam championships. Ryan won 17 doubles and nine mixed doubles titles between 1914 and 1934. Nineteen of her doubles titles came at Wimbledon.

9. **SUZANNE LENGLEN**

Suzanne Lenglen won 25 Grand Slam championships, all at Wimbledon and the French Open. Practically unbeatable between 1919 and 1926, she won 12 singles, eight women's doubles, and five mixed doubles titles in Grand Slam tournaments.

10. **STEFFI GRAF**

Despite winning only one Grand Slam doubles title, Steffi Graf won 23 Slam events between 1987 and 1999. Her 22 women's Grand Slam singles titles rank second to Margaret Smith Court.

Most Tournament Victories: Men

The players on this list are the all-time leaders in men's singles titles.

1. JIMMY CONNORS

The only male player to win more than a hundred singles titles was Jimmy Connors. He compiled 109 tournament victories between his first singles title in Jacksonville in 1972 and his final one in Tel Aviv in 1989. Connors was also a finalist in 54 other tournaments.

2. IVAN LENDL

Ivan Lendl won 94 singles titles during his career. Lendl was ranked the world's number-one player four times between 1985 and 1989. In the early 1980s, he had an indoor winning streak of 66 matches in a row. Lendl won eight Grand Slam singles titles and was a finalist in 19 Grand Slam events.

3. JOHN McENROE

John McEnroe won 77 singles titles during his career that lasted from 1977 to 1993. He was the number-one-ranked men's player from 1981 to 1984. In 1984, McEnroe lost only three matches all year. McEnroe also won 77 men's doubles championships.

4. PETE SAMPRAS

Pete Sampras has won 63 singles titles and a record 13 Grand Slam tournament victories. Both of those totals are likely to grow. Seven of his singles titles came at Wimbledon.

5. BJORN BORG

Despite retiring from tennis at age 27, Bjorn Borg won 62 singles titles. Between 1974 and 1981, Borg won six French Opens and five Wimbledon championships. He was also a four-time finalist at the U.S. Open.

6. GUILLERMO VILAS

Guillermo Vilas won 15 of his 62 singles titles in 1977. During one stretch, the Argentine won 44 consecutive matches. Between 1977 and 1979, Vilas won four Grand Slam singles titles.

7. ILIE NASTASE

Ilie Nastase was one of the premier men's players of the 1970s. His total of 57 singles victories would have undoubtedly been higher had not he so often lost his concentration due to his court antics. He was the number-one-ranked men's player in 1972 and 1973.

8. BORIS BECKER

Blessed with a booming serve and powerful volley, Boris Becker won 49 singles titles. His power game was ideally suited to Wimbledon where he won three singles championships between 1985 and 1989.

9. ROD LAVER

The only player to win tennis's Grand Slam twice, Rod Laver won 47 singles titles during his career. Laver was the top-ranked men's player in 1961, 1962, 1968, and 1969.

10. ANDRE AGASSI

Andre Agassi won more than 40 tournaments during the 1990s, and that total should continue to grow. The flamboyant Agassi has come back from tennis oblivion in the late 1990s to return to his position as one of the best players in the world.

Most Tournament Victories: Women

M artina Navratilova heads a list of women's winningest players.

1. **MARTINA NAVRATILOVA**

The 162 singles victories of Martina Navratilova are the most in tennis history. Nine of these victories came at the most revered of all tournaments, Wimbledon. She was ranked as the number-one woman player in 1978, 1979, 1982, 1983, 1984, 1985, and 1986.

2. **CHRIS EVERT**

Martina Navratilova's great rival, Chris Evert, is all-time second in singles victories with 154. Her invincibility on clay courts is evidenced by her 125 match winning streak and her seven French Open titles. She proved that she could win on any surface by notching six U.S. Open wins.

3. STEFFI GRAF

Steffi Graf won 22 Grand Slam singles titles and 105 overall. Although she had such great players as Martina Navratilova and Monica Seles as her contemporaries, Graf was ranked number one for a record 374 weeks.

4. MARGARET SMITH COURT

With a record two dozen Grand Slam singles titles and 92 career tournament victories, Margaret Smith Court was one of tennis's greatest winners. Her win total would have been even higher had she not taken breaks during three pregnancies. Seven times between 1962 and 1973, she ended the year ranked as the number-one player in women's tennis.

5. BILLIE JEAN KING

No one was more competitive than Billie Jean King. She racked up 67 singles titles during her long career that spanned from the early 1960s to early 1980s. Six times she accepted the trophy as Wimbledon champion.

6. EVONNE GOOLAGONG

Despite playing in an era that included Margaret Court, Billie Jean King, Chris Evert, and Martina Navratilova, Evonne Goolagong won 65 singles titles. Seven of her victories came in major championships.

7. VIRGINIA WADE

The greatest British women's player of the modern era, Virginia Wade won 55 singles titles. The 1968 U.S. Open

Steffi Graf waves to fans at Roland Garros during the 1999 French Open. Graf would win the tournament, her last Grand Slam title, and then retire August 13, 1999, with a number three ranking. While a number three ranking may not seem reason to retire for most, it apparently was for Graf, who had been ranked number one a record 374 total weeks during her career.

champion climaxed her career with an emotional victory at the 1977 Wimbledon Championships.

8. MONICA SELES

Monica Seles won more than 40 singles titles during the 1990s, even though she missed two years after being stabbed in 1993 by a deranged spectator. A nine-time Grand Slam winner, Seles was the top-ranked women's player in 1991 and 1992.

9. CONCHITA MARTINEZ

Spanish star Conchita Martinez has quietly amassed more than 30 singles titles. The pinnacle of her career was a dramatic victory over nine-time champion Martina Navratilova in the 1994 Wimbledon women's championship match.

10. TRACY AUSTIN

Plagued by injuries, Tracy Austin retired prematurely, yet still managed to win 29 tournaments during her brief career. Austin was the U.S. Open champion in 1979 and 1981.

The Greatest Men Players

From Willie Renshaw to Pete Sampras, there have been many great men tennis players. Henri Cochet, René Lacoste, Fred Perry, Jack Kramer, Pancho Gonzales, Frank Sedgman, Lew Hoad, John Newcombe, and Andre Agassi all left their marks on the sport.

1. ROD LAVER

You could make a strong case for several players as the best male tennis player of all time. Bill Tilden, Pete Sampras, and Jimmy Connors all have their supporters, but the name most often mentioned is Rod Laver. A player with few, if any, weaknesses, he is the only person ever to win the Grand Slam twice.

2. PETE SAMPRAS

Pete Sampras is tennis's all-time money winner with prize money exceeding 40 million dollars. His victory in the 2000 Wimbledon men's final against Patrick Rafter gave Sampras his seventh Wimbledon title and, more importantly, a record thirteenth Grand Slam singles title. Others have played more exciting tennis, but few can match his record.

3. ROY EMERSON

He was not as overwhelming as Rod Laver, as charismatic as John Newcombe, or as beloved as Ken Rosewall, but Roy Emerson won more major championships than any of his famous countrymen. Emerson's record of 12 Grand Slam singles titles is second only to Pete Sampras's, and his 28 total Grand Slam victories is a record in men's tennis.

4. BJORN BORG

Bjorn Borg was known as the "Ice Man" because he rarely showed emotion during his matches. With ice water in his veins, Borg more than held his own with his animated rivals, John McEnroe and Jimmy Connors. Borg won six French Opens and five Wimbledon championships before his early retirement at age 27.

5. BILL TILDEN

Bill Tilden was considered the greatest male tennis player of the first half of the twentieth century. A player with virtually no weaknesses, Tilden was the undisputed king of tennis during the 1920s. "Big Bill" won seven U.S. Opens and three Wimbledon titles.

6. JIMMY CONNORS

Jimmy Connors was not only one of the most exciting players in tennis history but also one of the most successful. His 109 career singles titles are the most achieved by a male player. His aggressive play was most often rewarded at the U.S. Open where he was a five-time champion. His best year was 1974 when he won Wimbledon, the U.S. Open, and the Australian Open.

7. DON BUDGE

Don Budge was the first player to win tennis's Grand Slam. The red-haired American accomplished this feat in 1938. From 1937 to 1938, Budge won six consecutive Grand Slam singles titles. Having accomplished all that he could as an amateur, he turned professional in 1939.

8. JOHN McENROE

John McEnroe won 77 singles and 77 men's doubles titles during his career. A gifted player with a great touch, McEnroe was the world's number-one-ranked player from 1981 to 1984. The controversial left-hander won four U.S. Opens and three Wimbledon singles crowns.

9. IVAN LENDL

Ivan Lendl methodically mowed down his opponents with powerful strokes and dogged determination. The Czech star won 94 singles titles and eight Grand Slam championships. He was the number-one-ranked player four times during the late 1980s.

10. KEN ROSEWALL

Ken Rosewall was one of the most popular players of all time. He showed that a player with style and finesse could defeat more powerful rivals. Unlike most players, Rosewall's skills did not lessen with age. A Grand Slam champion at age 18, Rosewall was nearly 40 when he last reached the finals of the U.S. Open in 1974. He won eight Grand Slam singles and nine doubles titles.

The Greatest Women Players

From Charlotte Dod to Venus Williams, there have been many great female players.

1. SUZANNE LENGLEN

From 1919 to 1926, Suzanne Lenglen lost only one singles match, a 1921 U.S. Open match against Molla Mallory in which Lenglen was too ill to continue. Lenglen was the closest thing to perfection the game of tennis has known. In a tournament at Nice, France, she won five matches by 6–0, 6–0 scores. Prior to the Wimbledon tournament in the early 1920s, Lenglen contracted jaundice. Despite being ill, she won three matches without losing a game. A perfectionist, she once became violently ill after losing two games in a match. Although she retired at age 27, Lenglen won 81 singles and 73 doubles titles. In seven years at Wimbledon, Lenglen lost only three sets. Lenglen won six Wimbledon and six French Open singles titles.

2. **MARGARET SMITH COURT**

Margaret Smith Court brought a power game to women's tennis. No player had a better record in Grand Slam tournaments. She won 24 singles, 19 doubles, and 19 mixed doubles titles in Grand Slam events. Eleven times she was the Australian Open women's champion, and seven times she reigned as the U.S. Open champion. In 1970, she achieved the ultimate by winning tennis's Grand Slam.

3. **MARTINA NAVRATILOVA**

Martina Navratilova won 56 Grand Slam titles, including 18 singles titles. Her 31 women's doubles titles in Grand Slam tournaments are by far the most taken by any player. Navratilova's powerful serve-and-volley game and intensity proved too much for most opponents. Navratilova won a record 167 tournaments, and during a period from 1984 to 1985, she won four Grand Slam tournaments in succession. Her greatest legacy is nine Wimbledon singles titles.

4. **STEFFI GRAF**

Steffi Graf used her blistering forehand to win 22 Grand Slam and 105 singles titles. She is the only player ever to win each of the Grand Slam singles titles at least four times. In 1988, Graf not only won the Grand Slam, but she was the gold medalist in tennis at the Seoul Summer Olympic Games. Not a bad year for a 19 year old.

5. **CHRIS EVERT**

Chris Evert won 154 singles titles—thanks to her hard groundstrokes and highly competitive nature. A model of consistency, she won by making fewer mistakes than her opponents. In her first seven years as a professional, Evert never lost two matches in a row. She won 125 consecutive matches on clay, her favorite surface. From 1974 to 1986, she won at least one Grand Slam singles title every year. Evert retired with 18 Grand Slam singles titles, six of which came at the U.S. Open.

6. **HELEN WILLS MOODY**

Helen Wills Moody played at Wimbledon for nine years and came away women's champion eight times. Over one six-year period, she did not lose a set at Wimbledon or the U.S. Open. "Little Miss Poker Face" won eight Wimbledon and seven U.S. Open singles titles. For nine years between 1927 and 1938, she was the top-ranked women's player.

7. **MAUREEN CONNOLLY**

Maureen Connolly was only 16 years old when she won her first French and U.S. Open titles in 1951. In 1953, Connolly became the first woman to win the Grand Slam. As a teenager she won nine Grand Slam titles before a serious leg injury suffered during a horse riding accident ended her career.

8. **BILLIE JEAN KING**

Billie Jean King was probably the player most responsible for helping to raise the status of women's tennis to equal that of men's. Her victory against Bobby Riggs in the Battle of the Sexes match in 1973 helped women achieve equal prize money in tournaments. Skilled at both singles and doubles, King won 39 Grand Slam titles, including a record 20 at Wimbledon.

9. **MONICA SELES**

One can only guess how many Grand Slam titles Monica Seles would have won had she not been stabbed in the back by a fan in 1993. She won eight Slam titles before the attack and has taken only one since.

10. **MARIA BUENO**

The player who raised tennis to an art form was Maria Bueno. The graceful Brazilian was a darling with tennis fans in the early 1960s. Besides being a joy to watch, Bueno managed to win four U.S. Open and three Wimbledon singles championships.

Tennis's Greatest Feats

Chris Evert won 125 consecutive matches on clay. Martina Navratilova and Pam Shriver won 109 doubles matches in a row. Rod Laver won tennis's Grand Slam twice. Here are some more of tennis's greatest achievements.

1. MARTINA NAVRATILOVA

For most players, winning one Wimbledon singles title is a dream. Martina Navratilova won nine Wimbledon women's singles titles. She won six in a row from 1982 to 1987.

2. WILLIE RENSHAW

Martina Navratilova was not the first player to win six consecutive Wimbledon singles. A century before, Willie Renshaw won six consecutive Wimbledons from 1881 to 1886.

3. BILL TILDEN

Bill Tilden won six consecutive U.S. Opens from 1920 to 1925. In all six finals, he defeated his rival, Bill Johnston.

4. BJORN BORG

From 1976 to 1980, Bjorn Borg won five consecutive Wimbledon titles. He was denied a sixth in 1981 when he lost a five-set match in the finals to John McEnroe.

5. MARGARET SMITH COURT

With Margaret Smith Court, it's hard to choose a greatest achievement because she had so many. She won 24 Grand Slam singles and 62 Grand Slam titles. Her record at the Australian Open is without peer. She won 11 Australian Open singles titles and an incredible seven in a row from 1960 to 1966.

6. LOUISE BROUGH and MARGARET DU PONT

The team of Louise Brough and Margaret du Pont dominated women's tennis in the 1940s and 1950s. Their most awesome achievement was to win the women's doubles competition at the U.S. Open 12 times.

7. MOLLA MALLORY

Who holds the record for the most U.S. Open singles titles? The answer is Molla Mallory. She won eight U.S. Open championships between 1915 and 1926.

8. SUZANNE LENGLEN

Suzanne Lenglen won five consecutive Wimbledon singles titles from 1919 to 1923. Her greatest play may have come at the 1925 Wimbledon championship. En route to victory, Lenglen lost only five games in five matches.

9. ROY EMERSON

Roy Emerson won five consecutive Australian Opens from 1963 to 1967. He won six of the seven finals he played in between 1961 and 1967.

10. IVAN LENDL

Ivan Lendl played in eight consecutive men's singles finals at the U.S. Open from 1982 to 1989. Lendl was the U.S. Open champion in 1985, 1986, and 1987.

Court Artists

Some players perform with such grace and fluidity that the game rises to the level of an art form. Rafael Osuna and Manuel Orantes were two players whose artistry on the court was a joy to watch.

1. MARIA BUENO

No one ever played the game of tennis more beautifully than Maria Bueno. For Bueno, it was not enough to win a point, it had to be won artfully. Her obsession with playing the perfect point may have cost Bueno matches, but it made watching her matches an unforgettable experience. The number-one-ranked women's player in 1959 and 1960, Bueno won seven Grand Slam titles.

2. HENRI COCHET

Henri Cochet was described as a tennis genius. His racket was a magic wand, pulling off seemingly impossible shots. The stylish Frenchman won four French

Opens, two Wimbledon championships, and a U.S. Open title between 1926 and 1932.

3. SUZANNE LENGLEN

Suzanne Lenglen was a ballerina on the court. She leaped and twirled as she swatted balls out of the air. Rivals complained that Lenglen jumped when it was not necessary, just to put on a show for the spectators. Her acrobatic play was actually the inspiration for the choreography of a ballet by composer Claude Debussy.

4. EVONNE GOOLAGONG

Evonne Goolagong seemed to float across the court. One of the most graceful players in tennis history, Goolagong could hit shots from any angle. Occasionally, she had a lapse of concentration, which she referred to as a "walkabout." Goolagong won seven Grand Slam singles titles.

5. HANA MANDLIKOVA

Few players were blessed with the natural talent that Hana Mandlikova possessed. When she was on, nobody played the game better. Mandlikova could hit spectacular winners from anywhere on the court. Unfortunately, she was not always able to maintain her brilliant play. Although she won the 1985 U.S. Open and three other Grand Slam singles titles, Mandlikova never attained the greatness many believed she would reach.

6. **ILIE NASTASE**

It seemed that Ilie Nastase had every shot in the book. As much an entertainer as an athlete, Nastase often seemed more concerned with hitting a crowd-pleasing shot than with winning a match. The highlight of Nastase's career was a victory over Arthur Ashe in the men's singles finals of the 1972 U.S. Open.

7. **ROSEMARY CASALS**

Rosemary Casals possessed almost too many shots for her own good. Because she had so many types of shots she could hit, Casals had more choices to make than players with a limited repertoire. Her varied game suited her best in doubles, where she formed one of the most successful teams in women's tennis with Billie Jean King.

8. **HENRI LECONTE**

One of the most stylish players of the 1980s and 1990s, Frenchman Henri Leconte was a master shotmaker. The left-hander was sometimes inconsistent, but his unpredictability made watching him even more enjoyable.

9. **GABRIELA SABATINI**

Gabriela Sabatini was not only one of the most attractive tennis players but also one of the most exciting to watch. A perfect combination of athleticism and grace, Sabatini won the women's singles title at the United

States Open in 1990 and was a finalist at Wimbledon in 1991.

10. **ARTHUR ASHE**

Arthur Ashe was the thinking man's tennis player. Ashe outwitted and outplayed most of the best players of his day. The man with the picture-perfect backhand was the U.S. Open men's champion in 1968 and the winner at Wimbledon in 1975.

Forgotten Greats

Many of tennis's early stars are little known today. All of these players deserve to be recognized for their remarkable careers.

1. MOLLA MALLORY

Born in Norway, Molla Mallory emigrated to the United States in 1914 when she was 30 years old. She had her greatest success in the United States, winning a record eight U.S. Open singles championships between 1915 and 1926.

2. WILLIE RENSHAW

Willie Renshaw was tennis's first dominant men's player. The Englishman won six straight Wimbledon singles titles from 1881 to 1886 and added a seventh in 1889. He and twin brother, Ernest, also combined to win seven Wimbledon men's doubles championships between 1880 and 1889.

3. DICK SEARS

Dick Sears won the first U.S. Open men's singles championship in 1881. He played in seven U.S. Opens and won them all. Sears also won the men's doubles title at the U.S. Open for six straight years from 1882 to 1887. Sears used a lopsided racket in the early years, a carry-over from an earlier form of the game called real tennis.

4. BILL LARNED

Bill Larned is one of three men to have won seven U.S. Open men's singles titles, the others being Dick Sears and Bill Tilden. Larned won the Open title in 1901, 1902, 1907, 1908, 1909, 1910, and 1911.

5. DOROTHEA CHAMBERS

Few players have had a greater impact on women's tennis than Dorothea Chambers. She won more than 200 tournaments during her career and went undefeated in five separate years. Chambers was the women's champion at Wimbledon seven times between 1903 and 1914. After her playing days were over, she became an outstanding tennis coach.

6. BLANCHE BINGLEY

Blanche Bingley had one of the longest and most successful careers. She won six Wimbledon women's singles titles between 1886 and 1900. Bingley reached the finals at Wimbledon 13 times and was a semifinalist at age 41 in 1912.

7. CHARLOTTE COOPER

At the turn of the twentieth century, the best women's tennis player in the world was Charlotte Cooper of Great Britain. Cooper won the Wimbledon women's singles title five times between 1895 and 1908.

8. TONY WILDING

Tony Wilding of New Zealand won the Wimbledon men's singles title for four consecutive years from 1910 to 1913. Known for his daring play, Wilding was a crowd favorite. He was in his prime when World War I began. Wilding joined the British Royal Marines and was killed in action in France on May 19, 1915.

9. WILFRED BADDERLEY

Wilfred Badderley was 19 years old when he won his first Wimbledon men's singles title in 1891. A finalist at Wimbledon for six consecutive years, Badderley also won the men's singles championship in 1892 and 1895. Wilfred teamed with his twin brother, Herbert, to win four men's doubles titles between 1891 and 1896.

10. NORMAN BROOKES

Norman Brookes was the first player from outside the British Isles to win a men's singles title at Wimbledon.

The Australian made the breakthrough at the 1907 Wimbledon championship. In 1914, at age 37, Brookes won his second Wimbledon title. In 1939, Brookes was awarded a different kind of title when he was knighted.

The Grand Slam and Beyond

S ome tennis tournaments stand out from the rest.

1. WIMBLEDON

Wimbledon has become synonymous with tennis. It is the tournament with the longest history and the most prestige, and it is the tournament that players most want to win. After Goran Ivanisevic fulfilled his dream of winning Wimbledon in 2001, he said that he did not care if he ever won another tournament. Martina Navratilova, who won a record nine women's singles titles, described winning Wimbledon as an addiction, satisfied only by another championship. In 1868, the All England Croquet Club was formed. Seven years later, a court was built for the new game of lawn tennis. The Wimbledon's men's championship was inaugurated in 1877, and the women's competition began in 1884.

Wimbledon is the only Grand Slam tournament still played on grass. Martina Navratilova, Helen Wills Moody, Pete Sampras, Steffi Graf, Billie Jean King, Suzanne Lenglen, and Bjorn Borg are among the players who have won five or more singles titles at Wimbledon. Clay court specialists may hate Wimbledon—even Ivan Lendl has said, "Grass is for golf." Nevertheless, few can dispute that Wimbledon holds a special place in the hearts of most tennis players and fans.

2. U.S. OPEN

If the U.S. Open is not the greatest tournament in the world, it's not far behind. The men's tournament began in 1881, and the first women's competition took place in 1887. Over the years, the tournament has been played on a variety of surfaces. It is now played on hard courts. From 1921 to 1977, the tournament was played in Forest Hills, New York. From 1974 to 1978, the tournament was played on three different surfaces. In 1978, the Open was moved to a bigger facility at Flushing Meadow, New York. Bill Tilden, Jimmy Connors, Chris Evert, Margaret Smith Court, and Steffi Graf all won five or more singles championships at the U.S. Open.

3. FRENCH OPEN

In recent years, the French Open has been the most unpredictable of the four Grand Slam tournaments.

The only one played on clay, it gives clay court specialists their best chance at a major title. Many hard court specialists have been unable to win on the slower clay surface at Roland Garros. The Paris tournament has existed since 1891. Chris Evert, Bjorn Borg, Steffi Graf, and Suzanne Lenglen all won the French Open six times or more.

4. THE AUSTRALIAN OPEN

The Australian Open is the first Grand Slam tournament of the year. The Melbourne tournament was first played in 1905, but the women's competition was not started until 1922. The tournament has grown in stature over the last 20 years, after being considered the weakest link in the Grand Slam for a number of years. In the past, many players skipped the tournament because it was played during the Christmas season and it required long jet flights to get there. Margaret Smith Court's 11 Australian Open singles titles is by far the most by any player.

5. ITALIAN OPEN

The Italian Open is played in Rome in the spring and has been considered by many to be a fifth major tournament. Although it may have lost a little of its stature in recent years, the Italian Open is still a coveted title. Recent winners of the Italian Open include Venus Williams and Gustavo Kuerten.

6. TENNIS MASTERS CINCINNATI

Another tournament that has attained a status just
below Grand Slam level is the Tennis Masters Cincinnati. The men's tournament, played in Mason, Ohio,
just prior to the U.S. Open, always attracts a world class
field. Formerly known as the ATP Championship, the
tournament has been won by most of the top players
of the past two decades including Pete Sampras,
Michael Chang, Boris Becker, and Stefan Edberg.

7. FEDERATION CUP

The Federation Cup is the women's equivalent of the
Davis Cup. The competition, which was first held in
1963, matches teams from different nations. The annual
competition has been dominated by the United States.
Other countries that won the cup include Australia,
Spain, Czechoslovakia, Germany, France, and South
Africa.

8. WIGHTMAN CUP

The Wightman Cup was an annual competition
between women players from the United States and
Great Britain. The Wightman Cup was first held in 1923
and continued until 1989. The main reason for its
demise was American dominance. The Americans held
a 51-10 advantage at the time the competition was dis-
continued. Another factor was the growing popularity
of the Federation Cup.

9. **ATP WORLD CHAMPIONSHIP**

The ATP World Championship is a year-end competition bringing together the top men players in Frankfurt, Germany. Winners of the tournament have included Pete Sampras, Andre Agassi, Boris Becker, and Michael Stich. From 1970 to 1989, a similar tournament, the Masters, was held in New York. John McEnroe, Jimmy Connors, Bjorn Borg, Ilie Nastase, Ivan Lendl, Boris Becker, and Stefan Edberg were among the winners.

10. **WTA TOUR CHAMPIONSHIP**

Since 1972 the WTA (World Tennis Association) Tour has conducted an annual championship featuring the best women tennis players in the world. The tournament was originally known as the Virginia Slims Championship, bearing the name of the women's tour sponsor. Some of the champions to win the event were Chris Evert, Evonne Goolagong, Martina Navratilova, Tracy Austin, Steffi Graf, Gabriela Sabatini, Monica Seles, and Martina Hingis.

The Davis Cup

The Davis Cup was begun in 1900 by a young American player named Dwight Davis who donated the silver trophy. It is an annual event that matches men's teams from many nations, and it has helped popularize tennis throughout the world. In many countries, the Davis Cup is tennis's premier event. The United States has won more than 30 Davis Cups, the most of any nation. Other countries that have won the Davis Cup include Australia, France, Sweden, Great Britain, Germany, Czechoslovakia, Italy, and South Africa. Here are some of the most memorable moments in Davis Cup history.

1. THE FIRST DAVIS CUP

The first three Davis Cups were limited to teams from the United States and Great Britain. The first country other than Great Britain and the United States to win the Davis Cup was Australia in 1907.

2. HANS REDL

Austrian tennis player Hans Redl lost his left arm during the siege of Stalingrad in World War II. Despite the handicap, Redl competed in the Davis Cup for Austria from 1948 to 1955. Rather than toss the ball into the air on his serve, Redl flipped the ball off his racket. Redl was able to win a singles match and three doubles matches during his Davis Cup competition.

3. BUSTER MOTTRAM

The December 1978 Davis Cup match between Great Britain's Buster Mottram and Brian Gottfried of the United States was memorable because of the adverse weather conditions. It was an unusually cold day in Palm Springs, California, and icicles hung from the lemon trees. Mottram defeated Gottfried in five sets, but it was Britain's only victory, as the United States won four matches to one.

4. WILMER ALLISON

Wilmer Allison of the United States and Giorgio de Stefani of Italy played one of the most dramatic matches in Davis Cup history on July 18, 1930. Allison saved an incredible 18 match points and rallied from two sets down in a 4–6, 7–9, 6–4, 8–6, 10–8 victory.

5. HAROON RAHIM

The youngest player ever to compete in the Davis Cup was Haroon Rahim of Pakistan. He was 15 in 1965 when he competed in a Davis Cup match against Vietnam in Kuala Lumpur. Rahim defeated Von Van Bay 3–6, 3–6, 7–5, 7–5, 6–1. It was Pakistan's only victory in a 4–1 loss to Vietnam.

6. WILBUR COEN

Wilbur Coen holds the distinction of being the youngest American to represent the United States in the Davis Cup. He was 16 when he competed in the 1928 Davis Cup. The United States reached the finals but lost to France.

7. HARRY FRITZ

One of the longest singles matches in Davis Cup history occurred between Harry Fritz of Canada and Jorge Andrew of Venezuela. Fritz won the marathon match 16–14, 11–9, 9–11, 4–6, 11–9.

8. STAN SMITH and ERIK VAN DILLEN

A 1973 doubles match between Stan Smith and Erik Van Dillen of the United States and Jaime Fillol and Pat Cornejo of Chile had a set that lasted 76 games. Smith and Van Dillen prevailed 7–9, 37–39, 8–6, 6–1, 6–3.

9. NICOLA PIETRANGELI

Nicola Pietrangeli of Italy had one of the most impressive records in the Davis Cup. He competed for Italy from 1954 to 1972. His record in singles matches was 78-32, and he was 42-12 in doubles.

10. **SOUTH AFRICA**

South Africa's participation in the Davis Cup resulted in numerous protests. In 1969, demonstrators protesting South Africa's policy of apartheid threw bags of flour on the court during a match against Great Britain played at Bristol, England. Great Britain won the match 3–2.

Going for the Gold

Tennis was an Olympic sport from 1896 to 1924. For 60 years tennis was excluded from the Olympics. It was reinstated as a medal sport at the 1988 Seoul Summer Olympics.

1. GUUS KESSLER

At the 1906 Athens Olympics, Guus Kessler won three matches without winning a game. He won his first three matches by default. In the fourth round Kessler lost to Max Decugis of France by the score of 6–0, 6–0. Decugis went on to win the gold medal, and Kessler did not medal.

2. GORDON LOWE

The second-round match between Gordon Lowe of Great Britain and Anasthasios Zerlentis of Greece at the 1920 Antwerp Olympics lasted nearly six hours. The match was so long that at one point the ballboys left the court to have lunch. Play was suspended, and the match was completed the next day. Lowe won the match 14–12, 6–8, 5–7, 6–4, 6–4. Worn out by his lengthy match, Lowe failed to reach the medal round.

3. SIGRID FICK

Sigrid Fick turned out to be her partner's worst enemy in a mixed doubles match at the 1912 Stockholm Olympics. The Swedish team of Sigrid Fick and Gunnar Setterwall met the German pair, Dora Koring and Heinrich Schomburgk, in the gold medal match. During the first set, the Swedish team was playing very well until Fick accidentally hit Setterwall in the face with her racket. The dazed Swede played poorly after being struck, and the Germans won the gold medal with an easy 6–4, 6–0 victory.

4. MARC ROSSET

The 1992 Barcelona Olympics men's singles field was one of the strongest ever assembled. Contenders for the gold medal included Pete Sampras, Boris Becker, Stefan Edberg, Jim Courier, Michael Stich, Michael Chang, and Thomas Muster. Amazingly, none of these players even medaled. The surprise gold medalist was Marc Rosset of Switzerland. In the gold medal match he defeated another lightly regarded player, Jordi Arresse of Spain, by the score of 7–6, 6–4, 3–6, 4–6, 8–6.

5. JOHN PIUS BOLAND

John Pius Boland, an Irish student at Christ's College in England, was invited by a Greek friend to visit Athens to be a spectator at the first modern Olympics in 1896. Once in Athens, Boland decided to enter the tennis competition. Amazingly, Boland won the gold medal in the men's singles competition. Boland also teamed with German Fritz Traun to win the men's doubles. Traun had come to Athens to compete in the 800-meter run and entered the tennis competition as an afterthought.

6. MAX DECUGIS

The most successful tennis player in Olympic history was Frenchman Max Decugis. At the 1906 Athens Olympics, Decugis won gold medals in the men's singles, men's doubles, and mixed doubles. In the mixed doubles, he teamed with his wife, Marie. Decugis won his fourth gold medal in the mixed doubles at the 1920 Antwerp Summer Olympics.

7. KITTY GODFREE

Kitty Godfree of Great Britain won five medals during her Olympic career. At the 1920 Antwerp Olympic Games, Godfree won a gold medal in the women's doubles, a silver medal in the mixed doubles, and a bronze in the women's singles. Four years later at the

Paris Summer Olympics, Godfree won the silver medal in the women's doubles and a bronze in the women's singles.

8. **LAURIE DOHERTY**

Brothers Laurie and Reggie Doherty were scheduled to meet in the semifinals of the men's singles competition at the 1900 Paris Olympics. Reggie stepped aside to let Laurie reach the gold medal match unopposed. Laurie Doherty won the gold, then teamed with Reggie to win the gold medal in the men's doubles.

9. **VENUS WILLIAMS**

Venus Williams of the United States defeated Elena Dementieva of Russia 6–2, 6–4 to win the women's singles medal at the 2000 Sydney Summer Olympics. Venus Williams won a gold medal with sister, Serena, in the women's doubles.

10. **GEORGE HILLYARD**

George Hilllyard of Great Britain was 44 years old when he teamed with Reggie Doherty to win the men's doubles gold medal at the 1908 London Olympics. Hillyard and Doherty defeated Josiah Ritchie and James Parke in the finals 9–7, 7–5, 9–7.

Dual Citizenships

Sometimes tennis nationalities can be blurred. Each of these players was born in one country but played for another.

1. MARTINA NAVRATILOVA

Martina Navratilova was born in Prague, Czechoslovakia, in 1956. She defected to the United States in 1975 while playing in the U.S. Open. Navratilova played for the United States in numerous Federation Cups and even led the American team to a victory over Czechoslovakia in 1986.

2. MARTINA HINGIS

Martina Hingis was born in Kosice, Slovakia, in 1980. She moved to Switzerland when she was seven years old. By March 1997, Hingis had risen to the rank of number-one women's player in the world.

3. **MARY PIERCE**

In 1975, Mary Pierce was born in Montreal, Canada. As a youth, Pierce lived and played tennis in the United States. Unhappy with her progress, her family decided to have her play for France. The switch was possible due to the French citizenship of her mother. In 1995, Pierce became the first Frenchwoman to win the Australian Open.

4. **YANNICK NOAH**

Yannick Noah grew up in Cameroon. He was 10 years old when he was discovered by Arthur Ashe, who was visiting the area. Noah returned to France, where he had been born, and developed into one of the best men's players of the 1980s. The high point of his career was a victory in the French Open in 1983.

5. **BOB HEWITT**

Bob Hewitt was born in Australia in 1940. Hewitt began his career playing for Australia, but he never represented his native country in the Davis Cup. Unhappy with the restrictions placed on players by the Australian tennis federations, in the 1960s Hewitt moved to South Africa, the native country of his wife. He became one of the best doubles players in tennis, winning nine Grand Slam men's doubles titles between 1961 and 1979.

6. **ALEX OLMEDO**

Alex Olmedo was born in Arequipa, Peru, on March 24, 1936. He won the Australian Open and Wimbledon championships in 1959. Olmedo chose to play in the Davis Cup for the United States because Peru did not have a Davis Cup team at the time. However, his selection for the American team was controversial because he had not been born in the United States.

7. **YVON PETRA**

Yvon Petra was born in French Indochina (which later became Vietman) in 1916. Petra played for France in the Davis Cup and twice won the men's doubles at the French Open.

8. **GREG RUSEDSKI**

Born in Montreal, Canada, in 1973, hard-serving Greg Rusedski adopted British nationality because his mother was born there. In 1995, Rusedski was a U.S. Open finalist. His top-five ranking was the highest ever for a British male tennis player.

9. **GUY FORGET**

Guy Forget was born in Casablanca, Morocco, in 1965. A highlight of his career was a victory against American Pete Sampras as he led France to their first Davis Cup victory in 59 years.

10. **MARY JOE FERNANDEZ**

Mary Joe Fernandez was born in the Dominican Republic in 1971. She moved to Florida and became a top player in both singles and doubles. She teamed with Gigi Fernandez to represent the United States in the Olympics. They won the gold medals in women's doubles at the 1992 Barcelona and 1996 Atlanta games.

Players Who never Won a Grand Slam Title

The highlight of most players' careers is a singles title at a Grand Slam tournament. However, some of tennis's best players were unable to win a Grand Slam title.

1. PAM SHRIVER

Pam Shriver appeared to be on her way to many Grand Slam titles when she reached the women's finals of the 1978 U.S. Open at age 16. Shriver lost the championship match to Chris Evert and never again reached another Grand Slam singles finals. As a doubles player Shriver had enormous success, winning 21 Grand Slam doubles titles.

2. ROSEMARY CASALS

Rosemary Casals was a finalist in the women's singles competition at the U.S. Open in 1970 and 1971, and four times she was a semifinalist at Wimbledon. Casals had the misfortune of competing at the same time as Margaret Smith Court, Billie Jean King, and Evonne Goolagong. Nevertheless, she excelled in doubles, winning nine Grand Slam titles.

3. **TOM OKKER**

Tom Okker lost a five-set match to Arthur Ashe in the finals of the 1968 U.S. Open. It was the closest that the Dutchman ever came to winning a Grand Slam singles title, although he reached the semifinals in all four Grand Slam tournaments. During his career, Okker won more than 20 singles titles.

4. **MARY JOE FERNANDEZ**

Mary Joe Fernandez reached the finals of three Grand Slam tournaments but lost all three. Fernandez was a finalist at the Australian Open in 1990 and 1992, and reached the championship match of the 1993 French Open. She was able to win the women's doubles titles at both the Australian and French Opens.

5. **BRIAN GOTTFRIED**

Brian Gottfried won more than two dozen singles titles. He was a finalist at the 1977 French Open and a semifinalist at Wimbledon in 1980. Gottfried did win the men's doubles titles at Wimbledon and the French Open.

6. **TODD MARTIN**

Todd Martin was always a feared opponent in Grand Slam tournaments. Martin pulled off many upsets over the years but never won a Grand Slam tournament. A finalist at the 1994 Australian Open, Martin also reached the semifinals at Wimbledon and the U.S. Open.

7. **BETTY STOVE**

Betty Stove won 20 singles titles and was the most successful Dutch woman in tennis history. She reached the finals of the women's singles at Wimbledon in 1977, but she lost to Virginia Wade. Stove did win three doubles titles at the U.S. Open between 1971 and 1979.

8. **CEDRIC PIOLINE**

Cedric Pioline may not be a household name, but the Frenchman did reach the finals of two Grand Slam tournaments. At the 1993 U.S. Open, Pioline lost in the men's finals to Pete Sampras. Four years later, he lost again to Sampras in the championship match at Wimbledon.

9. **EDDIE DIBBS**

Eddie Dibbs won 22 singles titles but never a Grand Slam. Frequently ranked in the top ten, he was a semifinalist at the French Open in both 1975 and 1976.

10. **HELENA SUKOVA**

Helena Sukova was twice a finalist in Grand Slam tournaments. The 6' 2" Czech lost to Chris Evert in the finals of the 1984 Australian Open, and she was runner-up to Martina Navratilova at the 1986 U.S. Open. Sukova was a four-time winner of the women's doubles at Wimbledon.

Players Who Never Won at Wimbledon

Wimbledon is the most prestigious tournament in the world. At the 2001 Wimbledon championships, Goron Ivanisevic proved that the third time is a charm. He had lost to Pete Sampras in the men's singles at Wimbledon in 1994 and 1998. In 2001, Ivanisevic capped his career with a five-set victory over Patrick Rafter in the Wimbledon's men's singles finals. The following players were not so fortunate.

1. KEN ROSEWALL

No player was more frustrated at Wimbledon than Ken Rosewall. He first reached the finals in 1954 as a 19 year old and lost a tough four-set match to Jaroslav Drobny. The Australian then lost to countryman Lew Hoad in 1956. He was unable to play at Wimbledon for many years in his prime because he was a professional. Rosewall took John Newcombe to five sets before losing in the 1970 men's finals. His fourth and final championship match was in 1974, when the 39-year-old Rosewall lost to Jimmy Connors.

2. IVAN LENDL

The only Grand Slam tournament that Ivan Lendl did not win was Wimbledon. Lendl lost to Boris Becker in the 1986 Wimbledon men's finals and the next year was runner-up to Pat Cash. Lendl was a five-time semi-finalist at Wimbledon.

3. FRED STOLLE

Fred Stolle was a finalist at Wimbledon in 1963, 1964, and 1965. In 1963, Stolle lost in the men's singles finals to Chuck McKinley. He lost to Roy Emerson in both the 1964 and 1965 championship matches.

4. HANA MANDLIKOVA

Hana Mandlikova's powerful game seemed perfectly suited for Wimbledon, yet it was the only Grand Slam tournament she never won. Mandlikova said that winning Wimbledon had been her biggest ambition in tennis. In 1981, she reached the finals, then lost to Chris Evert. Mandlikova was a finalist in 1986 but lost to Martina Navratilova.

5. ARANTXA SANCHEZ VICARIO

The winner of more than two dozen singles titles, Arantxa Sanchez Vicario is a three-time French Open champion. She also won the 1994 U.S. Open when she defeated Steffi Graf in three sets. The Spaniard lost to Graf in the Wimbledon finals in 1995 and 1996.

6. ILIE NASTASE

The 1972 U.S. Open champion, Ilie Nastase was twice a finalist at Wimbledon. In 1972 Nastase lost to Stan Smith and five years later was defeated by Bjorn Borg.

7. PANCHO GONZALES

A tennis legend, Pancho Gonzales was the men's singles champion at the U.S. Open in 1948 and 1949. Gonzales turned professional in 1950 and never won at Wimbledon. If he had not been excluded from playing because of his status as a professional, he would almost certainly have won at Wimbledon.

8. ELIZABETH RYAN

Elizabeth Ryan's record of 19 Wimbledon titles is all-time second to Billie Jean King's. All of her titles came in women's doubles and mixed doubles competitions. Twice she reached the women's singles finals at Wimbledon. In 1921, she lost to Suzanne Lenglen. Ryan was defeated by Helen Wills Moody in the 1930 women's championship match.

9. GUILLERMO VILAS

Guillermo Vilas won 62 tournaments and four Grand Slam singles titles. In 1977, he won an incredible 15 tournaments. Vilas never advanced past the quarterfinals at Wimbledon.

10. **JIM COURIER**

Jim Courier reached the number-one ranking in the world in 1992. A two-time winner at both the French and Australian Opens, Courier never won the Wimbledon championship. He lost a four-set men's final at Wimbledon in 1993.

Players Who Never Won the U.S. Open

The U.S. Open is the premier tennis tournament in America. There have been some great players who never won at the Open.

1. BJORN BORG

Bjorn Borg is the greatest player never to win the U.S. Open. Borg won 11 Grand Slam titles between 1974 and 1981. The sensational Swede was a four-time finalist at the U.S. Open. In 1976 and 1978, Borg lost four-set matches to Jimmy Connors. He lost a classic five-set match to John McEnroe in 1980. The next year, Borg again fell to McEnroe, this time in four sets.

2. EVONNE GOOLAGONG

Evonne Goolagong won seven Grand Slam singles championships. The one major tournament she did not win was the U.S. Open. She played in the Open women's championship match four consecutive years from 1973 to 1976, and four times she came away the loser. In

1973, Goolagong lost a three-set match to Margaret Smith Court. The next year, she lost another three-setter, this time to Billie Jean King. She lost to Chris Evert in the finals of the 1975 and 1976 U.S. Opens.

3. **JIM COURIER**

American Jim Courier, a four-time Grand Slam champion, was never able to win his national title. He came closest in 1991 when he lost to Stefan Edberg in straight sets in the men's singles final.

4. **MICHAEL CHANG**

When 17-year-old Michael Chang won the 1989 French Open, it was assumed that it was just a matter of time before he won his first U.S. Open. He did reach the final at the 1996 Open but lost to Pete Sampras 6–1, 6–4, 7–6.

5. **NANCY RICHEY**

The winner of 25 tournaments, Nancy Richey was twice a finalist at the U.S. Open. In 1966, Richey lost in straight sets to Maria Bueno. She met the same fate three years later in a straight-set loss to Margaret Smith Court.

6. **VITAS GERULAITIS**

A native New Yorker, nothing would have pleased Vitas Gerulaitis more than to win a U.S. Open title. His best chance came in 1979 when he reached the men's final against another New Yorker, John McEnroe.

However, it was McEnroe who won *his* first U.S. Open with a 7−5, 6−3, 6−3 victory.

7. **TONY ROCHE**

Tony Roche twice reached the men's final at the U.S. Open only to lose to fellow Australians. Roche lost in four sets to Rod Laver in 1969. The next year he was a four-set loser to Ken Rosewall.

8. **ROSEMARY CASALS**

Rosemary Casals never won a Grand Slam singles title, but she made valiant efforts at both the 1970 and 1971 U.S. Opens. In 1970, Casals lost a tough three-set match to Margaret Smith Court. She came out on the short end of another tight three-setter the next year against Billie Jean King.

9. **LEW HOAD**

In 1956, Lew Hoad won the first three legs of the Grand Slam. He was denied the Slam when he lost in the finals of the U.S. Open to countryman Ken Rosewall 4−6, 6−2, 6−3, 6−3. Hoad turned professional and never again had the opportunity to win the U.S. Open.

10. **BOB LUTZ**

Bob Lutz won four U.S. Open men's doubles championships with partner, Stan Smith, between 1968 and 1980. A talented singles player, Lutz never won the U.S. Open men's title. In 1969 Lutz was a finalist for the U.S. Open amateur title.

While Pete Sampras's strong serve-and-volley game worked well on the grass at Wimbledon and the hard courts of the U.S. Open, it was less effective on the clay of the French Open, the one major title that eluded Sampras.

Players Who Never Won the French Open

T he French Open is the only Grand Slam tournament played on clay. Many hard court specialists, including some of the greatest players of all time, have failed in their attempts to win the French Open.

1. PETE SAMPRAS

Pete Sampras has won a record 13 Grand Slam men's singles titles. His strong serve-and-volley game have helped him win seven Wimbledon and four U.S. Open crowns. The one major title to elude him has been the French Open, where his power game is less effective.

2. BILL TILDEN

Bill Tilden dominated men's tennis in the 1920s. "Big Bill" won seven U.S. Open singles titles and three Wimbledon championships. He never won the French Open, although he did reach the finals on two occasions. In 1927, Tilden lost a heartbreaker to René

Lacoste. Tilden was beaten 11–9 in the fifth and deciding set. Three years later he lost to another Frenchman, Henri Cochet, in four sets.

3. JIMMY CONNORS

Five of Jimmy Connors's eight Grand Slam singles titles came in the U.S. Open. Another player who preferred fast surfaces to clay, Connors never reached the singles finals at the French Open.

4. JOHN McENROE

John McEnroe was another top American player who never tasted victory at the French Open. He won seven Grand Slam singles titles, but the best he could do at the French Open was a runner-up finish. In 1984 he seemed poised to win the title when he led Ivan Lendl two sets to none in the final. Uncharacteristically, McEnroe lost the last three sets and the match.

5. JOHN NEWCOMBE

John Newcombe won seven Grand Slam singles titles. He won the Australian Open, Wimbledon, and the U.S. Open at least twice each. The one that got away was the French Open. His serve-and-volley game was less suited for clay, and he never reached the finals at the French Open.

6. **MARIA BUENO**

Maria Bueno won four U.S. Open singles titles and three at Wimbledon. Her best showing at the French Open was a runner-up finish in 1964. Bueno lost in the ladies final to Margaret Smith (Court) by the score of 5–7, 6–1, 6–2.

7. **LOUISE BROUGH**

Louise Brough won four Wimbledon singles titles between 1948 and 1955. She won every Grand Slam singles title except the French Open. She was never a singles finalist at the French Open, but she did win three women's doubles titles there.

8. **FRANK SEDGMAN**

The winner of five Grand Slam singles titles, Frank Sedgman never won the singles title at the French Open. The closest he came was in 1952 when he lost the championship match to Jaroslav Drobny in four sets.

9. **BORIS BECKER**

Boris Becker's powerful serve carried him to three Wimbledon singles titles. His power was neutralized on the slower clay surface at Roland Garros, and the German never reached the men's final at the French Open.

10. NEALE FRASER

Australian Neale Fraser won three Grand Slam singles titles. Although he never won the men's singles title at the French Open, he did win three French Open men's doubles championships.

Never Number One: Men

The goal of every top tennis player is to be ranked number one. From 1914 to 1972, the London Daily Telegraph determined the unofficial number-one-ranked player. Since 1972, the rankings have been computed by the men's and women's tours. The following men are some of the great players who never reached the top spot in the rankings.

1. KEN ROSEWALL

Ken Rosewall won eight Grand Slam singles titles, but was never number one in the year-end world rankings. Rosewall was 40 years old when his ranking peaked at number two behind Jimmy Connors in 1975.

2. BORIS BECKER

Boris Becker was ranked in the top five from 1987 to 1993. The three-time Wimbledon champion was ranked second to Ivan Lendl in 1989 and to Stefan

Edberg in 1990. Although he did reach number one in January 1991, he never finished the year as the top-ranked men's player.

3. ARTHUR ASHE

Arthur Ashe won the two most prestigious tennis tournaments in the world, Wimbledon and the U.S. Open. Ashe never reached number one but was ranked number two in 1968 behind Rod Laver.

4. GUILLERMO VILAS

Guillermo Vilas was ranked number two behind Jimmy Connors in 1975. Two years later, Vilas won 15 tournaments, including the U.S. and French Opens. Despite the incredible year, Vilas was again ranked second to Connors.

5. MICHAEL CHANG

Michael Chang was ranked second to Pete Sampras in 1996. The following year Chang ranked behind only Sampras and Patrick Rafter.

6. TONY ROCHE

Tony Roche had the best year of his career in 1969 when he ranked second in the world. He had unfortunate timing, as top-ranked Rod Laver won the Grand Slam that year.

7. **PATRICK RAFTER**

Australian Patrick Rafter won the U.S. Open men's singles titles in 1997, but he was unable to displace Pete Sampras as the world's number-one player. Rafter was ranked number two in 1997 and fourth in 1998.

8. **MICHAEL STICH**

Michael Stich showed he was a world-class player when he won Wimbledon in 1991. His highest ranking occurred in 1993 when he was second to Pete Sampras.

9. **VITAS GERULAITIS**

Vitas Gerulaitis cracked the top ten when he was ranked fourth in 1977. He remained in the top five for the next two years.

10. **PAT CASH**

The highlight of Pat Cash's career was a win at Wimbledon in 1987. He was ranked seventh in 1987, the only time he ever placed in the top ten.

never number One: Women

All of these women were champions, but none reached the top-ranked spot.

1. ARANTXA SANCHEZ VICARIO

Three times Arantxa Sanchez Vicario was ranked second in the world behind her nemesis Steffi Graf. She was the number two player in 1993, 1994, and 1996. In 1994, she won both the U.S. and French Opens.

2. TRACY AUSTIN

Tracy Austin's stay near the top of the rankings was short but spectacular. The U.S. women's champion in 1979 and 1981, Austin was ranked number two to Chris Evert in 1980 and 1981.

3. VIRGINIA WADE

Virginia Wade defeated Billie Jean King 6–4, 6–2 to win the singles championship at the 1968 U.S. Open. Wade ranked second to King in the year-end rankings.

4. Ann Jones

Ann Jones was the 1969 Wimbledon women's champion. She finished the year ranked second to Margaret Smith Court.

5. Jana Novotna

Jana Novotna was ranked in the women's top ten throughout the 1990s. In 1997, Novotna was ranked behind only Martina Hingis. The next year Novotna won Wimbledon and was ranked third.

6. Conchita Martinez

Conchita Martinez's greatest moment in tennis was her victory against Martina Navratilova in the 1994 Wimbledon women's championship match. In 1995 Martinez reached number two, her highest world ranking.

7. Gabriela Sabatini

Gabriela Sabatini was ranked fifth in 1990, the year she won the U.S. Open. Sabatini was ranked third in 1989, 1991, and 1992.

8. Hana Mandlikova

Hana Mandlikova won four Grand Slam singles titles and undoubtedly would have won several more had she not played at the same time as two of the greatest players of all time, Martina Navratilova and Chris Evert. Mandlikova was ranked third in both 1984 and 1985, behind Navratilova and Evert.

9. **ANDREA JAEGER**

Andrea Jaeger's top ranking came in 1983. The young American was ranked third behind Martina Navratilova and Chris Evert.

10. **PAM SHRIVER**

Pam Shriver was ranked in the women's top ten from 1980 through 1988. She was ranked fourth in 1983, 1984, 1985, and 1987.

Embarrassing Losses

E ven great players have their off days. In the women's championship match of the 1926 French Open, three-time U.S. Open champion Mary Browne was routed by Suzanne Lenglen 6–1, 6–0. At the 1936 Wimbledon men's final, French Open champion Gottfried von Cramm was defeated by Fred Perry 6–1, 6–1, 6–0. Twenty-one-year-old Jimmy Connors humbled 39-year-old Ken Rosewall 6–1, 6–0, 6–1 in the men's singles final of the 1974 U.S. Open.

1. MISS HUISKAMP

The most one-sided match in tennis tournament history occurred in Seattle in 1910. A player identified as Miss Huiskamp lost every point in a 6–0, 6–0 loss to Hazel Hotchkiss.

2. MOLLA MALLORY

At the 1921 U.S. Open Molla Mallory handed Suzanne Lenglen her only loss between 1919 and 1926. The next time the two great players met was at the 1922 Wimbledon championships. Mallory's husband was so confident of another victory that he bet $10,000 on his wife. This time Lenglen dispatched Mallory 6–2, 6–0 in a match that lasted just 27 minutes. Six months later in a tournament in Nice, France, Lenglen trounced Mallory 6–0, 6–0.

3. KITTY MCKANE

Kitty McKane won her first Wimbledon singles title in 1924. The defending champion was overwhelmed by Suzanne Lenglen 6–0, 6–0 at Wimbledon in 1925.

4. MAUREEN CONNOLLY and JULIE SAMPSON

Maureen Connolly won the Grand Slam in women's singles in 1953. That year she suffered a disheartening defeat in the women's doubles finals at Wimbledon. Connolly and partner Julie Sampson lost 6–0, 6–0 to the team of Doris Hart and Shirley Fry. Connolly had defeated Hart in straight sets in the women's final.

5. HELEN FLETCHER and JEAN RINKEL

In the semifinals of the women's doubles at Wimbledon in 1953, Doris Hart and Shirley Fry proved too much for Helen Fletcher and Jean Rinkel. Hart and Fry won the match 6–0, 6–0. In their final two matches at Wimbledon in 1953, the team of Hart and Fry did not lose a game.

6. **DORA BOOTHBY**

In the 1910 Wimbledon women's singles finals Dora Boothby was defeated by Dorothea Lambert Chambers 6–2, 6–2. The two women also met in the 1911 Wimbledon championship match. Chambers was even more dominant as she crushed Boothby 6–0, 6–0.

7. **NATALIA ZVEREVA**

Natalia Zvereva was a fine singles player and superb at doubles. She met her match in the women's finals of the 1988 French Open. Zvereva did not win a game in a 6–0, 6–0 loss to Steffi Graf.

8. **HILDE SPERLING**

Hilde Sperling was overwhelmed 6–0, 6–0 by Alice Marble in the women's semifinals at Wimbledon in 1939. Marble lost only two games in the final, clinching her first Wimbledon title.

9. **SHIRLEY FRY**

Shirley Fry and Doris Hart were one of the greatest doubles teams in tennis history. The two friends met in the women's finals at Wimbledon in 1951. Hart showed her doubles partner no mercy as she disposed of her 6–1, 6–0 in only 34 minutes.

10. JOHN HARTLEY

Reverend John Hartley was the men's Wimbledon champion in 1879 and 1880. The reverend did not have a prayer against Willie Renshaw in the 1881 Wimbledon championship match. Hartley lost 6–0, 6–1, 6–1 in a match that lasted just 37 minutes.

Classic Collapses

For some players no lead is safe. Each of these play-ers had a match in their grasp only to let it slip away.

1. **JOSE HIGUERAS**

At the 1978 Italian Open, Jose Higueras of Spain led Italian Adriano Panatta 6–0, 5–1 and appeared to be on his way to an easy victory. He needed just one more game to advance to the next round. Heckled by the pro-Panatta crowd, Higueras completely collapsed and lost the match.

2. **JOHN McENROE**

John McEnroe was one of tennis's most feared com-petitors, but he let one get away in the championship match of the 1984 French Open against Ivan Lendl. McEnroe won the first two sets 6–3 and 6–2. He led the third set 4–3 and was up a break when Lendl staged a remarkable comeback. Lendl won the match 3–6, 2–6, 6–4, 7–5, 7–5 for his first Grand Slam singles title. Although McEnroe won seven Grand Slam singles titles, he never won the French Open.

3. BILL TILDEN

Bill Tilden won three Wimbledon championships, but he also experienced his most excruciating loss in the semifinals of the 1927 Wimbledon tournament against Henri Cochet. Tilden won the first two sets and led 5–1 in the third set when Cochet rallied. The Frenchman won the final three sets in a 2–6, 4–6, 7–5, 6–4, 6–3 come-from-behind victory. Cochet also came from two sets down in the championship match to defeat Jean Borotra 4–6, 4–6, 6–3, 6–4, 7–5.

4. MANUEL ORANTES

In the men's final of the 1974 French Open, Manuel Orantes of Spain won the first two sets from a Swedish teenager named Bjorn Borg. Orantes fell apart and won only two more games in the rest of the match in a 2–6, 6–7, 6–0, 6–1, 6–1 loss. It was the first of Borg's first French Open titles.

5. ROY EMERSON

Roy Emerson won 12 Grand Slam singles titles, but his most disappointing loss occurred in the finals of the 1962 French Open against countryman Rod Laver.

Emerson won the first two sets 6–3, 6–2 only to lose the last three by the scores of 6–3, 9–7, and 6–2.

6. JANA NOVOTNA

Jana Novotna was the victim of one of the most painful collapses in tennis history in the women's final against Steffi Graf. After splitting the first two sets, Novotna led Graf 4–1 in the third and deciding set. Novotna lost the last five games in a 7–6, 1–6, 6–4 loss. She was so distraught that she cried on the shoulder of the Duchess of Kent following the match.

7. BUDGE PATTY

Budge Patty was one point away from victory in a fourth-round match against Frenchman Robert Haillet at the 1958 French Open. He led 5–0 in the fifth and final set and was serving with a triple match point when he suddenly lost his touch. Patty lost seven consecutive games in a stunning defeat.

8. MRS. HOLCROFT-WATSON

A player identified as Mrs. Holcroft-Watson led Cissy Aussem 6–2, 5–2 in a 1928 French Open match. Aussem won 11 games in a row in a 2–6, 7–5, 6–0 victory.

9. FRANK PARKER

Frank Parker, the 1944 and 1945 U.S. Open champion, appeared ready to win his third men's singles title in the 1947 championship match against Jack Kramer. Parker won the first two sets 6−4 and 6−2, but Kramer swept the final three sets 6−1, 6−0, and 6−3.

10. **FRED STOLLE**

Fred Stolle lost in the 1964 Australian Open championship match to Roy Emerson. Stolle and Emerson met again in the 1965 Australian final. It looked as though Stolle would avenge his defeat as he won the first two sets from Emerson 9−7 and 6−2. Emerson rallied for a 7−9, 2−6, 6−4, 7−5, 6−1 victory.

All in the Family

Tennis can be a family affair. Over the years many families have produced more than one tennis star. Some of the most notable families in tennis include the McEnroes, Gulliksons, Lloyds, Stolles, and Jensens.

1. THE DOHERTY BROTHERS

The Doherty Brothers, Reggie and Laurence, were nick-named "Big Do" and "Little Do." The "Do" could have stood for domination as the brothers practically claimed Wimbledon as their own private tournament at the turn of the century. Reggie won the men's singles for four consecutive years from 1897 to 1900. Laurence won five consecutive men's championships from 1902 to 1906. The Doherty Brothers also won eight men's doubles titles at Wimbledon, and Reggie and Laurence won two gold medals each at the 1900 Paris Summer Olympics.

2. **THE RENSHAW BROTHERS**

Twin brothers Willie and Ernest Renshaw were nearly unbeatable during the 1880s. Willie Renshaw won six consecutive Wimbledon championships from 1881 to 1886, and he added a seventh men's title in 1889. Ernest won at Wimbledon in 1888. The Renshaw Brothers also won seven men's doubles titles between 1880 and 1889.

3. **THE WILLIAMS SISTERS**

The Williams sisters have already made their mark on the sport. Younger sister Serena was the 1999 U.S. Open women's champion, and Venus won back-to-back Wimbledon women's titles in 2000 and 2001.

4. **THE MALEEVA SISTERS**

Yulia Berberian was a nine-time Bulgarian women's champion and the mother of the Maleeva sisters. Manuela, the eldest, was ranked in the women's top ten from 1984 to 1992. She was a bronze medalist in women's singles at the 1988 Seoul Summer Olympics. Younger sister, Magdalena, was ranked in the top ten in 1995. The third sister, Katerina, was also a world class player. In 1993, all three were seeded at the Australian Open.

5. **THE ROOSEVELT SISTERS**

Grace and Ellen Roosevelt were first cousins to Franklin Delano Roosevelt, president of the United States from

1933 to 1945. Ellen won the women's singles title at the U.S. Open in 1890. Together the sisters won the women's doubles title at the Open that year.

6. nANCY and CLIFF RICHEY

Nancy Richey said of herself, "If looks could kill, I would have killed a number of people." A fierce competitor, Nancy won the U.S. Clay Court Championship six times. In 1968, she defeated Ann Jones to win the French Open. Richey was a finalist at the U.S. Open in 1966 and 1969. Equally adept at doubles, she was a women's doubles champion at Wimbledon, the U.S. Open, and the Australian Open. Brother Cliff was also a clay court specialist, winning the U.S. Clay Court Championships in 1966 and 1970. In 1970, Cliff Richey won eight tournaments and was ranked in the men's top ten.

7. THE BADDERLEY BROTHERS

Wilfred and Herbert Badderley were twin brothers who were among the best players of the 1890s. Wilfred won the Wimbledon's men's singles titles in 1891, 1892, and 1895. The Badderley Brothers reigned as men's doubles champions in 1891, 1894, 1895, and 1896.

8. TRACY and JOHN AUSTIN

Tracy Austin won the women's singles championships at the U.S. Open in 1979 and 1981. In 1980 Tracy teamed with her brother, John, to defeat Mark

Edmondson and Dianne Fromholtz 4–6, 6–4, 7–5 to win the mixed doubles title at Wimbledon. The Austins were the first brother-sister team to win the mixed doubles at Wimbledon. Sister Pam Austin was also an excellent player.

9. THE FORGETS

When Guy Forget won the Toulouse Open in France in 1986, he was the third generation of his family to do so. His grandfather and father also had won the tournament.

10. THE MAYER BROTHERS

Gene Mayer was a top-ten singles player in the early 1980s. His best year was 1980 when he won five singles titles. That year he teamed with his brother, Sandy, to win the Wimbledon men's doubles title.

Family Ties

Sometimes parents of tennis stars insist on making their presence felt.

1. **DAMIR DOKIC**

Damir Dokic, father of Yugoslavian-born women's tour player Jelena Dokic, has become as famous as his daughter due to his outrageous behavior. Jelena showed amazing promise at an early age. At 16, she upset number-one Martina Hingis in the first round at Wimbledon in 1999. The next year she reached the semifinals of Wimbledon, and in 2001 she won her first tournament. Despite Jelena's success, her father has usually been the center of attention.

At a tournament in Birmingham, England, in 1999, he was thrown out of the tournament for heckling his daughter's opponent. Unhappy with his treatment, he called the tournament officials "Nazis." After he was ejected, Dokic reportedly lay down in the road, blocking traffic, and then jumped on the hood of a car. At

Wimbledon, he smashed a reporter's cell phone following an interview. Other fits of misbehavior have included making an obscene gesture at a female reporter and accusing officials of rigging the draw against his daughter. At the 2000 U.S. Open, Dokic hurled a plate of salmon at a worker in the player's lounge cafeteria because he thought $10 was too much to pay for the small portion he had gotten. He was banned from the rest of the tournament and was suspended by the WTA for six months in 2001 for his inappropriate behavior.

2. **RICHARD WILLIAMS**

Richard Williams, the father of Venus and Serena Williams, has garnered his own share of the headlines with his unconventional approach to the game. He has claimed that racism still exists on the women's tennis tour, a charge Martina Hingis dismissed as "nonsense." Williams said that racism was a factor in his daughters being booed at a tournament in Indian Wells and reported that spectators had taunted him with racial slurs. Williams was accused of manipulating his daughters when Venus withdrew from the semifinal match against Serena at Indian Wells to give her younger sister an extra day of rest for the championship match. Williams denied that he ever interfered in his daughters' matches. His most infamous moment came at the 2000 Wimbledon championships. After Venus defeated Lindsay Davenport for her first Grand Slam title, her father danced in the player's box. Many observers thought the celebration was excessive and showed dis-respect toward Davenport. Martina Navratilova re-marked, "If he'd done that to me, I'd hit him." Williams said of himself, "When somebody says I'm crazy, I reply, 'You're right.'"

3. JIM PIERCE

Mary Pierce's career has been marred by controversies surrounding her father, Jim. Born in Montreal, Canada, Pierce began her tennis career in the United States. Her father felt Mary was being held back by the U.S. Tennis Federation, so he took advantage of his wife's French citizenship to allow his daughter to play for France. Sometimes his temper got out of control, and he was accused of abusive behavior toward his daughter, other players, coaches, and spectators. Eventually, Jim Pierce was banned from all venues on the WTA Tour.

4. CHARLES LENGLEN

Charles Lenglen, for better or worse, was an important influence on the development of his daughter, Suzanne, into one of the greatest women players of all time. He was never satisfied with her performance, even when she won by a score of 6–0, 6–0. He reward-ed and punished her in a way that some people use with their pets. When Suzanne played poorly, Charles would not put jam on her bread. When she hit a good shot, he would toss her brandy-soaked sugar cubes.

5. **PETER GRAF**

Peter Graf was an important factor in his daughter Steffi becoming a champion. He oversaw her early years on the tour and was accused of coaching her from the stands, a violation of the rules. Peter was later convicted of income tax evasion.

6. **STUART NUTHALL**

Stuart Nuthall was the father and coach of Betty Nuthall. He died in 1925 from complications resulting from anaesthesia during an operation for tennis elbow. Betty Nuthall was so devastated by her father's unexpected death that she retired from tennis. Fortunately, she returned to the game and won the women's singles at the 1930 U.S. Open.

7. **MIKE AGASSI**

Mike Agassi was a boxer for Iran in the 1952 Summer Olympics. He realized that his son, Andre, was gifted at tennis. He guided his son's early career and was known for his intensity. On one occasion, he broke Andre's trophy at a tournament in San Diego because his son finished second.

8. **CHARLOTTE COOPER'S FATHER**

Charlotte Cooper's father was the opposite of most tennis parents. While many parents take a hands-on approach to their children's careers, Charlotte's father was almost indifferent to her success. Cooper won five

Wimbledon women's singles titles between 1895 and 1908. Charlotte lived with her parents in a house a short distance from the Worple Road courts where Wimbledon was played. After she won her first Wimbledon championship, Charlotte returned home. Her father asked her where she had been. She replied that she had been playing in the Wimbledon final. "How did you do?", he asked. "I won," she replied. "I'm so glad," he said. End of conversation.

9. **VERA SUKOVA**

Vera Sukova was a finalist in women's singles at Wimbledon in 1962. She passed on her tennis ability to her daughter, Helena. Helena Sukova was a finalist at the 1984 Australian Open and at Wimbledon in 1986. She used her superb volley to help her win four Wimbledon women's doubles titles.

10. **JIMMY EVERT**

Jimmy Evert was an outstanding player in the 1940s. He was the winner of the 1947 Canadian Open. Evert became one of tennis's best coaches, and he developed many future champions at his Fort Lauderdale, Florida, training camp. His greatest pupil was his daughter, Chris. Under his tutelage, she became one of tennis's greatest champions. Chris Evert won 154 tournaments during her career, including 18 Grand Slam titles.

The Old College Try

The following NCAA (National Collegiate Athletic Association) men's tennis champions went on to tennis stardom.

1. PANCHO SEGURA

Born in Ecuador, Pancho Segura went to college at the University of Miami in Florida. Segura was the men's NCAA tennis champion in 1943, 1944, and 1945. He was the only player in the twentieth century to win three NCAA individual titles. Segura was a semifinalist at the U.S. Open all three years.

2. JOHN McENROE

John McEnroe was the NCAA men's tennis champion in 1978. That year he led Stanford to the team title. In 1979, McEnroe won his first Grand Slam title, the U.S. Open.

3. JIMMY CONNORS

In 1971, Jimmy Connors won the NCAA men's championship and led UCLA to the national intercollegiate title. His first Grand Slam title was the 1974 Australian Open.

4. ARTHUR ASHE

Another UCLA alumnus, Arthur Ashe was the 1965 men's champion. UCLA also won the team title that year. Ashe won the U.S. Open men's singles title in 1968.

5. TONY TRABERT

In 1951 Tony Trabert became the only player from the University of Cincinnati ever to win the NCAA men's singles tennis title. Three years later, Trabert won his first U.S. Open title.

6. DENNIS RALSTON

Dennis Ralston was the men's NCAA singles champion in 1963 and 1964 while attending the University of Southern California (USC). Ralston was a finalist at Wimbledon in 1966.

7. RAFAEL OSUNA

The 1962 NCAA men's singles champion was Mexican Rafael Osuna, who also played at USC. Osuna won the U.S. Open in 1963.

8. **STAN SMITH**

Yet another USC player to win the men's NCAA tennis title, Stan Smith led the Trojans to the team title in 1968. Smith was the 1971 U.S. Open men's champion.

9. **KEVIN CURREN**

Hard-serving Kevin Curren of the University of Texas was the 1979 NCAA men's champion. The highlight of his professional career was a runner-up finish at Wimbledon in 1985.

10. **ALEX OLMEDO**

Alex Olmedo of USC won the men's NCAA tennis title in 1956 and 1958. Olmedo was the champion at both Wimbledon and the Australian Open in 1959.

Love Matches

Anna Kournikova's love life has generated as much interest as her tennis. Here are ten more highly publicized tennis romances.

1. JIMMY CONNORS and CHRIS EVERT

Jimmy Connors and Chris Evert were the best young tennis players in America when their romance blossomed in the early 1970s. In 1974, the year they were engaged, Connors won the Australian Open, Wimbledon, and the U.S. Open. Evert won the women's singles titles at the French Open and Wimbledon. The pair was called the "Lovebird double." Evert and Connors planned to marry in November 1974, but in September they announced that the engagement was off.

2. ANDRE AGASSI and STEFFI GRAF

Today's equivalent of the Connors-Evert romance is the union of Andre Agassi and Steffi Graf. Agassi and Graf have won 30 Grand Slam singles titles between them. They knew each other for years, but their romance did not blossom until Graf retired in the late 1990s.

3. ANDRE AGASSI and BROOKE SHIELDS

Andre Agassi is the closest thing tennis has to a movie star. Therefore, it was not surprising that the charismatic Agassi married a movie star, the beautiful actress Brooke Shields, in 1997. (Her grandfather, Frank Shields, was a finalist at Wimbledon in 1931.) Agassi devoted more time to his marriage, and his tennis game suffered. His world ranking dropped as low as 130. The marriage was annulled in 1999, and, with his concentration focused again on tennis, Agassi returned to the top of the rankings.

4. JOHN McENROE and TATUM O'NEAL

Tennis bad boy John McEnroe met actress Tatum O'Neal at a party in 1984. O'Neal, the daughter of actor Ryan O'Neal, had won an Academy Award at age 10 for Best Supporting Actress for her role in *Paper Moon.* McEnroe and O'Neal married in 1986. McEnroe's tennis game suffered as he devoted more time to his wife and family. McEnroe, who was ranked number two in 1985, dropped out of the top ten the next year. O'Neal and McEnroe divorced in 1994. McEnroe never returned to the tennis form of his prime in the early 1980s.

Andre Agassi was involved in not one but two "love matches" during his career, marrying actress Brooke Shields in 1997 and fellow tennis superstar Steffi Graf in 2001, four days before the birth of their son. If Agassi and Graf had produced a daughter, promoter John Korff was set to offer $10 million for the girl to appear in his A&P Tennis Classic women's tournament in 2017.

5. JOHN McENROE and PATTY SMYTH

John McEnroe met rock star Patty Smyth at a Christmas party. Smyth had a top-ten hit, "The Warrior," as the lead singer of the rock group, Scandal, in 1984. McEnroe, who played guitar in his own rock band, married Smyth in 1997.

6. CHRIS EVERT and JOHN LLOYD

Although her romance with Jimmy Connors ended in 1974, Chris Evert did marry a tennis player a few years later. Evert married a handsome Englishman named John Lloyd. He could not match the success of his wife, but Lloyd was a finalist in the men's singles at the 1977 Australian Open and won the mixed doubles twice at Wimbledon with partner Wendy Turnbull. Evert's marriage to Lloyd lasted nearly a decade, and she later married skiing champion, Andy Mill, in 1988.

7. JIMMY CONNORS and PATTI MCGUIRE

Unlike his old flame Chris Evert, Jimmy Connors did not marry another tennis player. His choice was a stunning brunette, Patti McGuire, who was the 1977 Playmate of the Year. They married in 1979.

8. GOTTFRIED VON CRAMM and BARBARA HUTTON

Gottfried von Cramm was one of the best tennis players of the 1930s, winning the French Open championship in 1934 and 1936. The urbane German later became a member of the international jet set. In 1955, he married Barbara Hutton, the fabulously wealthy heir to the Woolworth fortune. They divorced in 1958.

9. GUILLERMO VILAS and PRINCESS CAROLINE

Argentine tennis star Guillermo Vilas had a brief romance with Monaco's Princess Caroline, the beautiful daughter of actress Grace Kelly. The royal family disapproved of the union, and the romance soon ended.

10. BORIS BECKER and ANGELA ERMAKOVA

Boris Becker's brief encounter with Angela Ermakova proved to be a costly one. In July 2001, the three-time Wimbledon champion reached a paternity suit settlement with the Russian model. According to Becker, he only met Ermakova once. He said in a German television interview that he had met her in Nobu, a London restaurant, following his defeat by Patrick Rafter at Wimbledon in 1999. Becker said that he performed a brief sexual act with Ermakova in a laundry cupboard at the restaurant. The result of the tryst was a daughter named Anna.

Battle of the Sexes

The famous 1973 Billie Jean King–Bobby Riggs match was not the first time men and women have competed on the court.

1. BILLIE JEAN KING and BOBBY RIGGS

The September 1973 "Battle of the Sexes" match between Billie Jean King and Bobby Riggs was the greatest spectacle in tennis history. More than 30,000 spectators viewed the event in person at the Houston Astrodome, while 50 million watched on television. The 55-year-old Riggs had challenged King to prove that a man well past his prime could still beat one of the best women players in the world. The 1939 Wimbledon champion, Riggs argued that women did not deserve the same prize money as men.

The match divided the tennis fans between the men rooting for Riggs and the women pulling for King. Rosemary Casals, King's doubles partner and an outspoken supporter of women's tennis, described Riggs as "an obnoxious has-been who can't hear, can't see, walks like a duck, and is an idiot." Riggs, mainly because of his thrashing of Margaret Court on Mother's Day, was installed as an eight to five favorite. Reportedly, Riggs bet heavily on himself. Billie Jean King was carried into the arena in a sedan chair on the shoulders of male bodybuilders. Riggs made his entrance in a rickshaw pulled by buxom women. King's strategy of making Riggs run as much as possible paid off as she won in straight sets 6–4, 6–3, 6–3. The match helped establish the women's tour and helped them achieve prize money equal to that of men.

2. **BOBBY RIGGS and MARGARET SMITH COURT**

The match that led to the Battle of the Sexes was the Mother's Day match in California between Bobby Riggs and Margaret Smith Court. Riggs, the self-proclaimed "King of the Male Chauvinist Pigs" challenged Court, the best women's player in the world. In 1973, Court won an incredible 18 tournaments, including three Grand Slam events. The master of mind games, Riggs presented Court with a bouquet of roses prior to the match. Using dinks and lobs, Riggs destroyed Court's timing. Before she knew what hit her, Riggs shocked Court 6–2, 6–1 in a match that became known as the Mother's Day Massacre. Following the match, Riggs proclaimed himself the champion of women's tennis. He asked, "What kind of tour is it if the best player can't beat a guy with one foot in the grave?"

3. **ERNEST RENSHAW** and **CHARLOTTE DOD**

The first Battle of the Sexes occurred in 1888 between Ernest Renshaw and Charlotte Dod. Renshaw, the Wimbledon men's champion, agreed to a handicap match against Charlotte Dod, the defending Wimbledon women's champion. The match was played in Exmouth, England. Renshaw let Dod have a 30–0 lead in each game. Dod won the first set 6–2. Renshaw rallied to win the final two sets 7–5, 7–5.

4. **BILL TILDEN** and **SUZANNE LENGLEN**

Bill Tilden and Suzanne Lenglen were the greatest male and female players of their time. On May 27, 1921, they played an exhibition match in Saint Cloud, France. Tilden took advantage of his powerful game to win the one-set exhibition 6–0. When the proud Lenglen was asked afterward who had won the match, she answered, "Someone won 6–0, but I don't recall who it was." The next day Lenglen got a measure of revenge when she teamed with Max Decugis to defeat Tilden and Arnold Jones 6–4 in a doubles exhibition.

5. **JIMMY CONNORS** and **MARTINA NAVRATILOVA**

In 1992 Jimmy Connors and Martina Navratilova played a match at Caesar's Palace in Las Vegas. Navratilova was given two serves to one for Connors, and his side of the court was four feet wider. Despite the advantages, Navratilova lost to Connors 7–5, 6–2.

6. JOHN McENROE and THE WILLIAMS SISTERS

In the late 1990s, John McEnroe said in an interview that Venus and Serena Williams lacked humility as well as respect for anyone in tennis, a strange charge considering McEnroe's past encounters with officials. Venus Williams refused to be drawn into the controversy. She said she did not even know McEnroe and had no opinion on his comments. McEnroe also suggested that the sisters could not beat him or any other player on the men's tour, but nothing came out of the challenge.

7. VITAS GERULAITIS

Vitas Gerulaitis, the 1977 Australian Open champion, showed little respect for players on the women's tour. In the 1980s, he said that any player on the men's tour could defeat the best women players. He issued a challenge to women players, but it was ignored.

8. RENEE RICHARDS

Renee Richards had the distinction of playing in the U.S. Open both as a man and a woman. Born Richard Reskind, he played in the men's singles of the U.S. Open in 1955. Twenty-two years later, following a sex change operation in 1975 and a name change, Renee Richards played in the women's draw of the Open. Richards was ranked as high as number 22 on the women's tour and reached the women's doubles finals with Betty Ann Stuart at the 1977 U.S. Open.

9. **MARGARET SMITH and KEN FLETCHER**

Men and women play together in tournaments in the mixed doubles events. In 1963, Australians Margaret Smith (Court) and Ken Fletcher won the Grand Slam in the mixed doubles.

10. **LESLIE and KITTY GODFREE**

In 1926, Kitty and Leslie Godfree of Great Britain became the only married couple to win the mixed doubles at Wimbledon. The Godfrees defeated Howard Kinsey and Mary Browne 6–3, 6–4.

They've Come a Long Way

As in most sports, women had a long struggle for equality in tennis.

1. LADY MARGOT

The first reference to a female tennis player was in 1427. Lady Margot was one of France's best players of jeu de palme, an early version of tennis. By all accounts, she could beat most men players.

2. MAUD WATSON

Maud Watson won the first women's singles title at Wimbledon in 1884. The women's competition did not begin until after the men's had concluded. Watson also won the championship the next year.

3. NELLIE HANSWELL

The first women's winner of the U.S. Open was Nellie Hanswell in 1887. The men's competition was held six years before a women's competition was added. It was not until 1924 that the men's and women's competition were held at the same venue. The men's competitions were originally held at The Casino in Newport, Rhode Island, while the women's event took place at the Philadelphia Cricket Club.

4. MISS CASEY

The first known women's tournament was the Irish Open in 1876 in Dublin. The men's tournament was played on the beautiful grass courts of the Fitzwilliam Club. The women's tournament was moved to a private grounds because it was decided that the men's court was too public for women to play. Only two women entered the tournament, and Miss Casey defeated Miss Vance in the only match.

5. HAZEL WIGHTMAN

Hazel Hotchkiss Wightman was the U.S. Open women's champion in 1909, 1910, 1911, and 1919. In 1923, she donated the trophy for the first Wightman's Cup, a women's competition between teams from the United States and Great Britain. Wightman led the Americans to a 7–0 victory in the first Cup.

6. RUTH TAPSCOTT

Ruth Tapscott set a fashion precedent at Wimbledon in 1928. The South African was the first woman to play there without stockings.

7. **LILI D'ALVAREZ**

Another fashion first at Wimbledon occurred in 1931. Lili D'Alvarez became the first woman to wear shorts at the championships. The Spaniard was a finalist at Wimbledon in 1926, 1927, and 1928.

8. **PAULINE BETZ**

Pauline Betz won four U.S. Open women's singles titles between 1942 and 1946 and was the Wimbledon champion in 1946. In 1947, the 27 year old discussed the possibility of a professional tour for women. She was immediately branded a professional by the United States Tennis Association (USTA) and banned from amateur competitions such as Wimbledon and the U.S. Open. Because a women's professional tour did not exist at the time, Betz, although still in her prime, was relegated to playing a few exhibitions with Sarah Palfrey Cooke and Gussy Moran.

9. **GLADYS HELDMAN**

On September 23, 1970, nine women tennis players gathered at the Houston, Texas, home of Gladys Heldman, the publisher of the magazine, *World Tennis.* Heldman and the others were outraged that men's prize money was three to nine times higher than women's at the same tournaments. The players signed symbolic one dollar contracts with the new World Tennis Association. The nine included Billie Jean King,

Rosemary Casals, Julie Heldman, Nancy Richey, Kerry Melville, Peaches Bartkowicz, Val Ziegenfuss, Kristy Pigeon, and Judy Dalton. The Virginia Slims Tour began in 1971, and within a couple of years the women's prize money was comparable to the men's.

10. BILLIE JEAN KING

Perhaps no woman was more responsible for securing women's equality in tennis than Billie Jean King. Her victory over Bobby Riggs in 1973 was instrumental in raising public awareness of women's tennis.

African American Stars

The Williams sisters are the latest African American stars in tennis history, but there have been many others.

1. ARTHUR ASHE

Arthur Ashe was a men's champion at Wimbledon and the U.S. Open, but his impact on tennis has far exceeded his impressive record as a player. Articulate and dignified, Ashe was a great ambassador for tennis. He was responsible for many young African Americans taking up the game. His untimely death in 1993 at the age of 49, the result of AIDS contracted through a blood transfusion, was an irreplaceable loss for tennis.

2. ALTHEA GIBSON

Althea Gibson was the first African American to win a Grand Slam tournament, but as a youth she experienced racial discrimination. She was not permitted to play in the New Jersey State Championships. However, Gibson broke the color barrier at Wimbledon in 1950. At the age of 29, she won the French Open. She won both Wimbledon and the U.S. Open in 1957 and 1958 and was ranked number one in the world. In 1959 she retired from tennis and signed a $100,000 contract to play exhibitions at the halftimes of Harlem Globetrotters basketball games. Gibson later played on the women's professional golf tour. She was inducted into the International Tennis Hall of Fame in 1971.

3. VENUS WILLIAMS

In 2001, Venus Williams joined Althea Gibson as the only African American women to win Wimbledon twice. Venus also was the women's champion at the 2000 U.S. Open. In 2000, she was the women's gold medalist in tennis at the Sydney Summer Games.

4. SERENA WILLIAMS

Serena Williams won the women's singles title at the U.S. Open in 1999. She teamed with her sister, Venus, to win the women's doubles at the 2000 Sydney Summer Olympics.

5. ZINA GARRISON

Zina Garrison defeated Hana Mandlikova to win the 1986 European Indoors. Garrison won two more tournaments in 1987. The next year she teamed with Pam Shriver to win the gold medal in women's doubles at the Seoul Summer Olympics. In 1989, Garrison was

Serena Williams pumps her fist during the defense of her 1999 U.S. Open championship the following year. Serena lost to Lindsay Davenport in the quarterfinals in 2000 but would team with the eventual winner—her sister Venus—to capture Olympic gold for women's doubles in the 2000 Sydney Summer Olympics.

ranked number four. At the 1990 Wimbledon championships, Garrison defeated Monica Seles and Steffi Graf on her way to the finals. In the championship match she lost to Martina Navratilova.

6. LORI McNEIL

Lori McNeil was another top African American women's player in the 1980s. In September 1986, McNeil defeated her close friend, Zina Garrison, in a tournament in Tampa, Florida, by the scores of 2–6, 7–5, 6–2. It marked the first time two African American women had competed in a tournament final. McNeil was also a top-ranked doubles and mixed doubles player.

7. LUCY SLOWE

The first African American woman to win a singles title was Lucy Slowe. She won a tournament in Baltimore in 1917.

8. TULLY HOLMES

Tully Holmes was the first African American man to win a tennis tournament. Holmes was the men's singles champion in Baltimore in 1918, 1921, and 1924.

9. CHANDRA RUBIN

Chandra Rubin was a top African American women's player of the 1990s. One of her most memorable matches occurred in the semifinals of the 1996 Australian Open against Arantxa Sanchez Vicario. Rubin won the marathon match 6–4, 2–6, 16–14. The third set lasted 2 hours and 22 minutes.

10. **LESLIE ALLEN**

In 1981, Leslie Allen became the first African American woman to win a tournament in more than 20 years. Allen reached a peak ranking in the women's top twenty.

Great Rivalries

G reat rivalries in tennis often make for exciting matches. Some players bring out the best in others. Some of the most memorable rivalries in tennis history include Jack Kramer vs. Pancho Gonzales, Roy Emerson vs. Fred Stolle, Rod Laver vs. Arthur Ashe, Bjorn Borg vs. John McEnroe, and Chris Evert vs. Evonne Goolagong. These rivalries are among the greatest in tennis history.

1. CHRIS EVERT and MARTINA NAVRATILOVA

The longest rivalry in tournament tennis history was between Chris Evert and Martina Navratilova. They first met in 1973. Evert won 11 of their first 12 matches. In the 1980s Navratilova won 13 matches in a row. In their careers, they met 80 times, with Navratilova holding a 43-37 edge. Navratilova led nine to four in Grand Slam finals.

2. **ROD LAVER and KEN ROSEWALL**

The friendly rivalry between Australian greats Rod Laver and Ken Rosewall made for some of the best matches in tennis history. Laver, the only player to win two Grand Slams, was the perfect combination of power and skill. Rosewall, with his great backhand and court coverage, was the perfect foil. Rosewall defeated Laver in the championship match of the 1968 French Open, and Laver returned the favor in 1969. Their greatest match may have been the 1972 WCT (World Championship Tennis) finals in which Rosewall outlasted Laver in five sets.

3. **JOHN McENROE and JIMMY CONNORS**

John McEnroe and Jimmy Connors were two of the most successful and volatile players of the 1970s and 1980s. The intense competitors had a genuine dislike for one another, and their matchups were explosive. Two of their most memorable matches occurred in the men's finals at Wimbledon. In 1982, Connors defeated McEnroe in five grueling sets. Two years later, McEnroe trounced Connors in straight sets 6–1, 6–1, 6–2.

4. **MARGARET SMITH COURT and BILLIE JEAN KING**

Margaret Smith Court and Billie Jean King combined to win more than one hundred Grand Slam titles. The tall, powerful Court was the ideal rival for the fiercely competitive King. Court usually came out on top, but the matches were always hard fought. At the 1965 U.S. Open, Court bested King 8–6, 7–5 in the women's final. Their best battle may have been the 1970 Wimbledon championship match, which Court won 14–12, 11–9.

5. **BILL TILDEN and BILL JOHNSTON**

Although the rivalry was one-sided, Bill Tilden and Bill Johnston were unquestionably the best American male players of the 1920s. The 6′1″ Tilden was known as "Big Bill," and Johnston, who was six inches shorter, was called "Little Bill." Johnston defeated Tilden in the final of the 1919 U.S. Open. From 1920 to 1925, the two Bills met in the U.S. Open men's finals each year. Six times they played, and six times Tilden won. "I can't beat the son of a bitch," Johnston said in frustration.

6. **HELEN WILLS MOODY and HELEN JACOBS**

The two Helens, Helen Wills Moody and Helen Jacobs dominated American women's tennis during the 1920s and 1930s. Although both denied there was a feud, it was difficult for each to hide their hard feelings. Two matches stand out in their long rivalry. In the 1933 U.S. Open women's finals, Jacobs led Moody 8–6, 3–6, 3–0 when Moody was forced to retire with an injury. When Jacobs put her hand on Moody's shoulder in a sympathetic gesture, Moody reportedly told Jacobs to take her hands off. At Wimbledon in 1938, Jacobs partially tore her Achilles tendon in a match against Jadwiga Jedzejowska. Despite the painful injury, Jacobs insisted on playing in the women's final against Helen Wills Moody. Moody showed little sympathy for her injured foe and dispatched her in straight sets.

7. STEFFI GRAF and MONICA SELES

Steffi Graf was the number-one-ranked women's player from 1987 to 1990. Monica Seles took over the number-one spot in 1991 and 1992. In 1992, Graf defeated Seles in the Wimbledon women's final. Seles got the best of Graf at the 1992 French Open and 1993 Australian Open. The rivalry was just heating up when a spectator, who hoped to ensure Graf's return to her number-one ranking, stabbed Seles during a tournament. In Seles's absence, Graf did return to the number-one ranking, which she held until 1996.

8. PETE SAMPRAS and ANDRE AGASSI

The two best American men's players of the 1990s were complete opposites. Pete Sampras was a workmanlike player who let his tennis racket do his talking. By contrast, the flamboyant Andre Agassi was always the center of attention. Sampras was sure and steady. Agassi was brilliant and unpredictable. In 1995 Agassi defeated Sampras in the men's finals at the Australian Open. Later that year Sampras defeated Agassi for the U.S. Open title.

9. **MAUREEN CONNOLLY and DORIS HART**

When Maureen Connolly was growing up, Doris Hart was her idol. The first time they played against each other was at the 1950 U.S. Open, in which the star-struck teenager was defeated by Hart. Before their rematch in the semifinals of the 1951 U.S. Open, Connolly's coach, "Teach" Tennant, lied and told her that Hart considered her a spoiled brat. Angered, Connolly won easily in straight sets. When Connolly learned the truth, she resumed her friendship with Hart. Connolly played Hart in the women's finals at Wimbledon in 1953 and at the U.S. Open in 1952 and 1953, and won all three matches.

10. **SUZANNE LENGLEN and ELIZABETH RYAN**

Suzanne Lenglen and Elizabeth Ryan were one of the best women's doubles teams of the 1920s, but they were intense rivals in singles. Ryan accused Lenglen of being a poser whose spectacular leaps on the court were purely for show. Lenglen once threw Ryan's clothes out of a locker room window. In the Wimbledon women's finals in 1921, Lenglen routed Ryan 6–2, 6–0.

Bjorn Borg took on John McEnroe in an epic match for the 1980 Wimbledon championship. Borg's fifth straight Wimbledon championship is one of the top matches of all time, due in part to the marathon 18–16 fourth-set tiebreaker won by McEnroe to send the match to the fifth and deciding set.

Memorable Matches

The 2001 U.S. Open quarterfinal match between Pete Sampras and Andre Agassi was the latest in a long line of tennis matches for the ages. These tennis matches stand the test of time.

1. BJORN BORG and JOHN McENROE

Bjorn Borg defeated John McEnroe 1–6, 7–5, 6–3, 6–7, 8–6 in the men's finals at Wimbledon in 1980. It was Borg's fifth consecutive Wimbledon title and his last. What will forever be remembered from the match was the epic fourth-set tiebreaker won by McEnroe 18–16. The next year McEnroe ended Borg's reign as Wimbledon champion with a four-set victory in the finals.

2. SUZANNE LENGLEN and HELEN WILLS

Suzanne Lenglen and Helen Wills were two of the greatest champions in women's tennis. Unfortunately, their careers barely overlapped. Lenglen was at the end of her career when they met at the Carlton Club in

Cannes, France, on February 16, 1926. The match was called "The Battle of the Century." The invincible Lenglen had lost only one singles match in seven years and was a six-time Wimbledon champion. Wills was already a three-time U.S. Open champion. The match generated such interest that royalty from England, Russia, Portugal, and Greece were in attendance. Spectators who could not buy a ticket watched from rooftops and from the tops of buses parked outside. Lenglen prevailed 6–3, 8–6 and promptly turned professional. As expected, Wills replaced Lenglen as the best women's amateur tennis player.

3. KEN ROSEWALL and ROD LAVER

Rod Laver and Ken Rosewall met many times during their careers, but the encounter that is most remembered was the 1972 WCT championship match in Dallas, Texas. The see-saw match showed both champions at the top of their games. When it was over, Rosewall won by the score of 4–6, 6–0, 6–3, 6–7, 7–6.

4. MARGARET SMITH COURT and BILLIE JEAN KING

Any time Margaret Smith Court and Billie Jean King played, fans were guaranteed outstanding tennis. The two champions outdid themselves in the 1970 Wimbledon women's finals. Court prevailed 14–12, 11–9 in a match that lasted nearly two and a half hours.

5. DON BUDGE and GOTTFRIED VON CRAMM

This match was played more than 60 years ago, but it is still talked about today. American Don Budge was matched against Germany's top player, Gottfried Von Cramm in the 1937 Davis Cup Interzone Final. Budge came back from a 4–1 deficit in the final set to defeat Von Cramm 6–8, 5–7, 6–4, 6–2, 8–6. Even the defeated Von Cramm admitted that it was the greatest match he had ever seen.

6. RENÉ LACOSTE and BILL TILDEN

Bill Tilden overpowered players with a cannonball serve and textbook groundstrokes. René Lacoste was a master strategist who was his most dangerous when he was on the defensive. Lacoste and Tilden's most memorable match occurred in the men's final of the 1927 French Open. Lacoste won the match in three tough sets 11–9, 6–3, 11–9.

7. ARTHUR ASHE and JIMMY CONNORS

The 1975 Wimbledon's men's final was Arthur Ashe's greatest moment. Ashe was 10 years older than the 22-year-old Connors, who was considered unbeatable at the time. He had won three Grand Slam tournaments the previous year and had destroyed Ken Rosewall in straight sets at both Wimbledon and the U.S. Open. Everyone expected Ashe to be Connors's next victim, but Ashe had other ideas. He used his experience to dismantle Connors 6–1, 6–1, 5–7, 6–4.

8. SUZANNE LENGLEN and DOROTHY LAMBERT-CHAMBERS

The 1919 Wimbledon match between Dorothy Lambert-Chambers and Suzanne Lenglen represented a changing of the guard. The 40-year-old Lambert-Chambers had been the Wimbledon women's champion in 1910, 1911, 1913, and 1914. Twenty-year-old Suzanne Lenglen was her heir apparent. Lenglen survived two match points to defeat Lambert-Chambers 10–8, 4–6, 9–7. It was the first of her six Wimbledon titles.

9. BJORN BORG and VITAS GERULAITIS

Few semifinal matches are remembered, but the 1977 Wimbledon's men's semifinal between Bjorn Borg and Vitas Gerulaitis was a classic. Few matches contain such high quality play. Borg, who was practically unbeatable at Wimbledon, prevailed in five thrilling sets 6–4, 3–6, 6–3, 3–6, 8–6.

10. JOHN McENROE and JIMMY CONNORS

The 1980 U.S. Open semifinal match between John McEnroe and Jimmy Connors marked the high point of their heated rivalry. Momentum swung back and forth. At one point McEnroe lost 11 games in a row. After nearly four hours of action, McEnroe won in a fifth-set tiebreaker. In the championship match, McEnroe defeated Borg in another five-set match.

Ultimate Upsets

H ere are ten incredible tennis upsets.

1. BORIS BECKER

It's now hard to imagine that Boris Becker, a three-time Wimbledon champion, once pulled off one of tennis's biggest upsets. Seventeen-year-old Becker became the first unseeded player to win the men's singles title at Wimbledon in 1985 when he defeated Kevin Curren 6–3, 6–7, 7–6, 6–4.

2. KURT NIELSEN

Kurt Nielsen of Denmark was twice a finalist at Wimbledon. Both times he was unseeded. In 1963, he upset number-one seed Ken Rosewall before losing in the championship match to Vic Seixas. He upset Rosewall again in 1955 and advanced to the final against Tony Trabert. Nielsen lost to Trabert in straight sets 6–3, 7–5, 6–1.

3. CHRIS LEWIS

Another unlikely finalist at Wimbledon was Chris Lewis of New Zealand. Lewis was ranked ninety-first in the world and was unseeded at Wimbledon in 1983. He pulled off a series of upsets and reached the men's final against John McEnroe. Lewis lost 6–2, 6–2, 6–2 and never again challenged for a Grand Slam title.

4. JENNIFER CAPRIATI

The ultimate comeback story was Jennifer Capriati's. A teenage sensation, Capriati left the game for years and was written off by most people. Returning with a new maturity, Capriati rose again to the top of the women's ranks. At the 2001 Australian Open, the twelfth-seeded Capriati won her first Grand Slam singles title. A few months later, she won her first French Open.

5. IVA MAJOLI

In one of the biggest upsets in tournament history, ninth-seeded Iva Majoli of Croatia upset top-seeded Martina Hingis 6–4, 6–2 in the women's finals at the 1997 French Open. The unexpected defeat cost Hingis the Grand Slam.

6. VIRGINIA RUANO PASCUAL

Hingis was victimized by unknown Virginia Ruano Pascual in the first round of Wimbledon in 2001. Pascual, ranked eighty-third in the world, shocked the number-one seed 6–4, 6–2.

7. KAREN SUSMAN

Both women finalists at Wimbledon in 1962 were surprises. Eighth-seeded Karen Susman defeated unseeded Vera Sukova 6−4, 6−4. The 19-year-old American never won another Grand Slam singles title.

8. OLGA MOROZOVA

In 1974, Olga Morozova became the first Soviet to reach the final at Wimbledon. The eighth seed upset number-one seed Billie Jean King in the quarterfinals. The Cinderella story ended in the finals when Morozova was brought back to earth by Chris Evert, 6−0, 6−4.

9. NICK BROWN

Nick Brown of Great Britain holds the distinction of being the lowest-ranked player in Wimbledon history to upset a seeded player. In 1991, Brown, ranked number 590 in the world, defeated tenth-seeded Goran Ivanisevic 4−6, 6−4, 7−6, 6−3.

10. FRED STOLLE

Unseeded Fred Stolle upset longtime nemesis Roy Emerson on his way to victory at the 1966 U.S. Open. Emerson had defeated Stolle in the Wimbledon men's finals in both 1964 and 1965. Stolle defeated another Australian, John Newcombe, 4−6, 12−10, 6−3, 6−4 in the championship match.

SPOILERS

The Grand Slam is tennis's greatest achievement. These players stopped the Grand Slam bids of some of the game's greatest players.

1. CHRIS EVERT

Chris Evert won 18 Grand Slam singles titles but never the Grand Slam. Twice she spoiled the Grand Slam attempts of her rival, Martina Navratilova. In 1983, Navratilova won the Australian Open, Wimbledon, and the U.S. Open. Evert stopped the Slam with a victory in the French Open. The next year Evert won the Australian Open to again keep Navratilova from the Slam.

2. KEN ROSEWALL

Ken Rosewall twice spoiled Grand Slam bids. In 1955, he stopped Tony Trabert's bid for the Grand Slam by winning the Australian Open. The following year Rosewall defeated Lew Hoad in four sets at the U.S. Open championship match to stop Hoad's Grand Slam bid.

3. KAREN SUSMAN

Margaret Smith Court won the Grand Slam in 1970. In 1962, her bid for a Grand Slam was halted by Karen Susman, who won her only Grand Slam singles title at Wimbledon.

4. LESLEY TURNER

Margaret Smith (Court) also won three of the four Grand Slam titles in 1965. The one that got away was the French Open. In the women's championship match, Smith was defeated by Lesley Turner 6–3, 6–4.

5. MERVYN ROSE

Ashley Cooper won the Australian Open, Wimbledon, and the U.S. Open in 1958. Another Australian, Mervyn Rose, won the French Open.

6. VIRGINIA WADE

Billie Jean King won three-fourths of the Grand Slam in 1972. The only major tournament that she lost was the Australian Open, which was won by Virginia Wade.

7. BILLIE JEAN KING

Billie Jean King was the spoiler in 1973. Margaret Smith Court won the Australian, French, and the U.S. Opens. King stopped Court's Slam bid with a victory at Wimbledon.

8. STEFAN EDBERG

Mats Wilander nearly won the Grand Slam in 1988. The only Grand Slam tournament that he did not win was Wimbledon. That tournament was won by fellow Swede Stefan Edberg.

9. STEFFI GRAF

Steffi Graf won the Grand Slam in 1988. Four years later, she stopped Monica Seles from winning the Grand Slam by winning at Wimbledon. In the women's final, Graf routed Seles 6–2, 6–1.

10. MONICA SELES

Monica Seles returned the favor to Steffi Graf in 1996. Seles won the Australian Open, keeping her rival from completing a second Grand Slam.

Tennis Believe It or Not

In the 1991 Wimbledon semifinals Stefan Edberg lost to Michael Stich without losing his serve. Edberg lost three tiebreakers 3–6, 7–6, 7–6, 7–6. At the 1977 Anaheim Junior Championships, Cari Hagey and Collette Kavanaugh played a point that lasted 51 minutes. The second set, won by Hagey 6–4, lasted 3 hours and 45 minutes. Finally, Hagey won the three-set match, which lasted five hours. This list features tennis's most unbelievable moments.

1. V. ST. LEGER GOULD

The 1879 Wimbledon men's final featured two players of opposite moral natures. John Hartley was a minister. His opponent, a mysterious player named V. St. Leger Gould, became the most infamous man in tennis history. Hartley defeated Gould 6–2, 6–4, 6–2. In 1907, Gould was sentenced to life imprisonment for the murder of a Dutch woman named Emma Levin, whose dismembered body was discovered in a trunk belonging to Gould. The former tennis champion died in the notorious Devil's Island prison in 1909.

2. **RICHARD WILLIAMS**

Twenty-one-year-old Richard Williams was aboard the ill-fated ocean liner *Titanic* on its maiden voyage in 1912. More than 1,500 people lost their lives when the ship sank after striking an iceberg in the North Atlantic. Williams clung to an overturned lifeboat before he was rescued. Doctors wanted to amputate his frozen legs, but Williams refused. The unsinkable Williams not only recovered but also became the U.S. Open men's champion in 1914 and 1916.

3. **TONY PICKARD**

A hungry linesman cost Tony Pickard a match against Ian Crookenden at the Italian Open in Rome. Pickard reached match point in the fourth set when it appeared that Crookenden hit the ball out. Unfortunately, the linesman left his post to get an ice cream from a passing vendor. The point did not count, and Pickard went on to lose the match.

4. **DOROTHY CAVIS-BROWN**

On June 22, 1964, Clark Graebner and Abe Segal played a match that Wimbledon lineswoman Dorothy Cavis-Brown found less than exciting. Brown fell asleep, and Graebner had to wake her so the match could continue. Graebner said later that he was afraid she had died.

5. Bunny AUSTIN and WILBUR COEN

On February 22, 1930, Englishman Bunny Austin and Wilbur Coen were scheduled to play in the semifinals of a tournament in Beaulieu, France. Austin arrived late, and Coen was upset with officials because they did not default the match to him. To show his disgust, Coen did not try in the first set and lost 6–0. Austin returned the favor by throwing the second set 6–0. Both men played their best tennis in the final set, which Austin won 8–6.

6. ULF SCHMIDT and GARDNAR MULLOY

The third-round match between Ulf Schmidt of Sweden and Gardnar Mulloy at the 1956 Masters Invitational Tournament in Jacksonville, Florida, was halted by rain with the score tied 3–3 in the first set. It was decided to move the match to a high school gymnasium 10 miles away. Much to their chagrin, the players found the conditions even more slippery than outside. The gym had been used for an ice show, and the floor was still slick. After a few points, Mulloy and Schmidt gave up and returned to the outdoor courts. Once they resumed, Mulloy won the match 5–7, 6–4, 6–4.

7. BRIAN GOTTFRIED and RAUL RAMIREZ

The championship men's doubles match at the 1976 Italian Open featured the team of Brian Gottfried and Raul Ramirez against John Newcombe and Geoff Masters. The May 30 match was suspended in the fifth set because of darkness. Schedule conflicts prevented the players from continuing the match the next day. The teams decided to conclude the match at the Grow Professional Doubles Championships in Houston on September 15. Gottfried and Ramirez won the match 7–6, 5–7, 6–3, 3–6, 6–3, three and a half months after it had begun.

8. **TORBEN ULRICH**

Torben Ulrich of Denmark wished he had not played American Bill Hoepner at the 1953 Pacific Coast Tournament in Berkeley, California. Irritated by his opponent's constant stoppage of play to tie his shoes or clean his glasses, Ulrich was trailing 4–1 in the second set when he could stand no more. He walked to the net, shook hands with Hoepner, and left the court. When asked why he retired from the match, Ulrich replied, "It just wasn't any fun."

9. **RON KAPP and WILL DUGGAN**

On March 12, 1988, Ron Kapp and Will Duggan had a 6,202 shot rally during a match in Santa Barbara, California. The 3-hour-and-33-minute rally ended when Kapp missed a forehand.

10. **TONY WILDING and NORMAN BROOKES**

Tony Wilding of New Zealand and Norman Brookes of Australia made short work of Arthur Gore and Herbert Barrett of Great Britain in a doubles match at the Kent Championships in England. Wilding and Brookes won 6–2, 6–1 in a match that lasted just 16 minutes.

Colorful Characters

Tennis has had its share of colorful players. John McEnroe, Ilie Nastase, Jimmy Connors, and Cliff Richey entertained and sometimes outraged fans with their court antics. Meet some of tennis's most interesting personalities.

1. FRANK KOVACS

Frank Kovacs was a finalist in the men's singles at the 1941 U.S. Open. Today he is best remembered for his outrageous court antics. He was known to jump into the stands to applaud himself if he hit a great shot. If he was displeased, he staged sit-down strikes during matches. If a plane flew overhead, he pretended to machine gun it with a tennis racket. Once while serving he tossed three balls into the air and hit the middle one for an ace.

2. FAUSTO GARDINI

The wild man of tennis was Italian Fausto Gardini. Nicknamed the "Vampire," Gardini liked to chew on tennis balls. His most bizarre moment came at the 1955 Italian Internationals. His opponent was another Italian, Beppe "The Little Bird" Merlo. With the score tied 4–4 in the fourth set, Merlo collapsed in pain with leg cramps. As he writhed in pain on the court, Gardini stood over him and looked at his watch. Under the rules, an injured player was given one minute to recover. Gardini gleefully counted off the seconds and celebrated his opponent's inability to continue.

3. JEAN BOROTRA

One of the famed French "Four Musketeers," Jean Borotra was the Wimbledon men's champion in 1924 and 1926. Borotra brought six black berets with him for each match. Whenever Borotra put on a new beret, his opponent knew that he was going to raise the level of his tennis. In a doubles match with partner Jacques Brugnon at Wimbledon in the early 1930s, Borotra, on the run, hit a shot that fell into the laps of two young women seated courtside. Borotra paused to kiss the ladies' hands, then leaped back onto the court to hit a winning volley.

4. SUZANNE LENGLEN

Suzanne Lenglen may have been the greatest woman tennis player of all time, and she was one of the most temperamental. Between games Lenglen sipped cognac from a silver flask. A perfectionist, she had little patience with officials when she believed they made a bad call. In a tournament on the Riviera, she argued a call on a foot fault. When the linesman did not respond to her insults, she realized he was deaf. Lenglen wrote a message and handed it to the linesman. No one knows what she wrote, but the man was so offended that he stormed off the court.

5. BOBBY RIGGS

Bobby Riggs was a good enough player in his prime to win Wimbledon and the U.S. Open, but he will always be remembered as tennis's greatest showman. His challenge match against Billie Jean King helped popularize the new women's tour and brought new fans to tennis. Riggs attributed his longevity to taking 415 vitamins a day. The ultimate hustler, Riggs played a match wearing an overcoat and galoshes. Another time he tied himself with a rope to his doubles partner.

6. GUSSY MORAN

Gorgeous Gussy Moran created a sensation when she wore lace panties at Wimbledon in 1949. She was always making news. At one press conference, during which she was fitted for her new tennis outfits, it was announced that her measurements were 37-25-37. At another press conference, she performed a striptease behind a semitransparent screen. To get psyched up for a match, she would visit the zoo and watch the lions.

7. JIM COURIER

Jim Courier was not your average tennis player. The winner of four Grand Slam titles between 1991 and 1993, Courier carried stacks of books with him. He enjoyed literature, particularly books written in French. When he won the Australian Open in 1992, he celebrated by taking a dip in Melbourne's Yarra River.

8. ART LARSEN

Art Larsen was the men's champion at the 1950 U.S. Open. He was nicknamed "Tappy" because he had the habit of tapping things for good luck. Larsen tapped on anything within reach, from the net to an opponent.

9. FRED PERRY

Fred Perry was the first player to win all four Grand Slam titles in a career. A master of mind games, he was known to verbally probe the weaknesses of his opponents to gain a psychological edge. He was so abrasive that even though he was an Englishman, he was not popular with Wimbledon officials. When he won Wimbledon in 1934, his opponent, Jack Crawford, was presented with a bottle of champagne. Perry was not even congratulated.

10. ION TIRIAC

Ion Tiriac was one of the most intimidating players in tennis history. The hulking, moustached Tiriac was a doubles partner with fellow Romanian Ilie Nastase. He once said of himself, "I am the best tennis player who cannot play tennis."

Biggest Controversies

Tennis has had its share of controversy.

1. BILL TILDEN

Bill Tilden was voted the greatest player of the first half of the twentieth century, but his reputation was compromised by morals charges related to his homosexuality. In 1946, Tilden was arrested and charged with contributing to the delinquency of a minor. He served seven months in jail. In 1949, Tilden violated his parole when he allegedly made advances to a hitchhiker. He was then made to serve an additional 10 months in prison. When Tilden died in 1953, he had less than a hundred dollars in the bank.

2. 1973 WIMBLEDON BOYCOTT

In 1973, the Yugoslav Tennis Federation suspended Nikki Pilic for not honoring a commitment to play in the Davis Cup. Pilic denied ever saying that he would play for Yugoslavia. When Wimbledon honored the Yugoslav Federation's ban of Pilic, 93 of the world's best men tennis players boycotted the tournament. Thirteen of the 16 men's seeds did not play. The winner of the depleted Wimbledon was Jan Kodes.

3. **MARTINA NAVRATILOVA'S GRAND SLAM**

The tennis Grand Slam consists of winning the Australian Open, French Open, Wimbledon, and the U.S. Open in the same year. In the 1980s, the International Tennis Federation offered a million dollar bonus for any player who won the Slam. In 1983, Martina Navratilova won Wimbledon, the U.S. Open, and the Australian Open. When she won the French Open in 1984, she claimed that she had won the Grand Slam because she had won four major tournaments in a row. There was much debate over the issue, but the International Tennis Federation decided to award Navratilova the million dollars.

4. **ANNA KOURNIKOVA VIRUS**

Anna Kournikova is admired as much for her good looks as for her tennis ability. Her photographs are much in demand on the Internet. In February 2001, an e-mail virus disrupted computers throughout the United States. An e-mail message promised recipients a photo of the comely Kournikova. When unsuspecting people opened the message, their computers were infected by a virus. The worm did not destroy information, but it did tie up computers by monopolizing e-mail.

Fans hoping to see an enticing photograph of Anna Kournikova when opening their e-mail in February 2001 were instead infected with a virus that tied up their computers.

5. JENNIFER CAPRIATI

Jennifer Capriati was a teen phenom when she burst onto the tennis scene in the early 1990s. Unrealized expectations and burnout caused her to quit tennis. In May 1994, Capriati was arrested on marijuana possession charges. She was arrested on another occasion for shoplifting. However, Capriati staged a remarkable comeback and in 2001 won the Australian and French Opens.

6. MARTINA NAVRATILOVA and JUDY NELSON

Martina Navratilova made headlines with her same-sex relationship with a woman named Judy Nelson. Their relationship lasted from 1984 to 1991. The highly publicized palimony suit filed by Nelson was settled out of court.

7. ROSELEENA BLAIR

Roseleena Blair, a 19-year-old tennis player at Alabama-Huntsville College, was declared ineligible to play in September 2000 because a nude photograph of her appeared in *Playboy.* The issue featured "Sexy Girls in Sports." The NCAA declared that she was not suspended for posing nude, but rather for appearing in a magazine that was not sports related. Blair's record in singles was 0-11.

8. JIMMY CONNORS

Jimmy Connors caused a furor at Wimbledon in 1977 when he refused to participate in the Parade of

Champions celebrating the tournament's centennial. The parade featured players who had won singles championships at Wimbledon. Connors, the 1974 men's champion, did not endear himself to the British by refusing to march in the parade.

9. AMELIE MAURESMO

Martina Hingis is a popular player who became the world's number-one ranked women's tennis player in 1997. A few years later she caused a controversy with her unflattering comments about a rising young French player named Amelie Mauresmo. Hingis remarked that the muscular Mauresmo lacked femininity.

10. SUZANNE LENGLEN

Suzanne Lenglen's tennis was so enchanting that heads of state frequently were in attendance during her matches. Great Britain's King George V and Queen Mary were in the stands in 1926 to see Lenglen play a doubles match. Lenglen was upset because the French Tennis Federation ordered her to play with a French player, Diddie Vlasto, in a match against Elizabeth Ryan, an Englishwoman who was Lenglen's usual doubles partner, and Mary Browne. Lenglen snubbed the king and queen by refusing to play.

Temper Tantrums

They were usually throwing fits or their rackets.

1. JOHN McENROE

John McEnroe was tennis's super brat. He said of him-self, "My biggest strength is that I don't have any weak-nesses." While he rarely lost tennis matches, he fre-quently lost his self-control. McEnroe's greatest battles were with the umpires and linesmen. If he felt his opponent was victimized by a bad call, he would inten-tionally lose the point. He won his first Wimbledon men's singles title in 1981, breaking Bjorn Borg's five-year run as champion. That year McEnroe was fined $6,000 for his unsportsmanlike behavior. McEnroe uttered the immortal words, "You cannot be serious" and "pits of the world." These phrases would be heard by many tennis officials during the rest of his career. Always known for his unique way with words, McEnroe was fined again in 1983 for calling his Czech opponent, Tomas Smid, a "communist bastard." At the 1987 U.S. Open, McEnroe was fined $7,500 and suspended for two months for temper tantrums and use of obscene language. McEnroe usually reserved his bile for officials, but he had a run-in with Boris Becker at the 1989 Paris Open. Becker had a coughing spell that McEnroe mocked. By the end of the three-set match (won by Becker), the two champions were yelling at each other. McEnroe proved that he had not mellowed at the 1990 Australian Open. During a match against Mikael Pernfors, McEnroe was disqualified in the fourth set for repeated conduct violations, including smashing his racket. Incredibly, it marked the first time McEnroe had been disqualified from a tennis match.

2. **EARL COCHELL**

The only tennis player to be banned for life because of unsportsmanlike conduct was Earl Cochell. In 1951, the 29-year-old Cochell, ranked seventh in the world, played Gardnar Mulloy in the U.S. Open. Cochell frequently stopped action during the match to argue calls with linesmen. As the match progressed, the crowd became more and more vocal in their displeasure with Cochell. Angered by the boos and catcalls, Cochell tried to climb into the umpire's chair so he could use the microphone to tell the crowd what he thought of them. Then Cochell began to lose points on purpose. He served underhanded and played left-handed. Not surprisingly, he lost the match to Mulloy 4–6, 6–2, 6–1, 6–2. Two days later, the executive committee of the United States Lawn Tennis Association voted to ban Cochell from competition for life.

3. **ILIE NASTASE**

Probably no player angered his opponents more often than Ilie Nastase. He infuriated them with his frequent stalling tactics and arguments with officials. In a notorious 1979 match at the U.S. Open against John McEnroe, Nastase's stalling tactics caused a near-riot, and resulted in his being disqualified. Amazingly, the two men went out to dinner after the match.

It was not the first time Nastase had been disciplined at the U.S. Open. In 1976, he was suspended for 21 days and fined $1,000 for use of obscene language and unsportsmanlike behavior in a match against Hans Joachim Pohmann of Germany. In a Davis Cup doubles match against Great Britain, Nastase made a remark that angered David Lloyd so much that Lloyd approached the net and the result was a near confrontation. Nastase's closest call with being physically harmed by an opponent came at the 1972 Rothman's International Tournament in London. In a match against Clark Graebner, Nastase stopped play for several minutes by arguing a call. The hulking Graebner called Nastase to the net and told him that he was going to smash his racket over his head if he didn't continue. For once, Nastase listened to reason.

It was not the only time that Nastase's maddening behavior nearly caused a player to resort to violence. Englishman Roger Taylor, a former boxer, once reminded Nastase of his fisticuff skills during one of their matches.

4. JEFF TARANGO

Jeff Tarango became more famous for his court histrionics than for his play. In October 1994, in a tournament played in Tokyo, Tarango was so angered after losing his serve in the third set of a match against Michael Chang that he dropped his shorts. Tarango's most infamous moment came at Wimbledon in 1995. During a third-round match against Alexander Mronz of Germany, Tarango stormed off the court and was disqualified because he questioned the impartiality of umpire Bruno Rebeuh. After the match, Tarango's wife, Benedicte, slapped Rebeuh to "teach him a lesson." Tarango was taught a lesson in court etiquette by being suspended from the next Grand Slam tournament and barred from playing at Wimbledon the next year.

5. GORAN IVANISEVIC

Goran Ivanisevic may hold the record for the most tennis rackets broken in a career. "I pay more fines for breaking rackets than some guys' career prize money," he joked. In November 2000, at the Samsung Open in

Brighton, England, he was forced to default a match because he had broken all his rackets in fits of anger. Ivanisevic once said that he would "be remembered as the guy who never won Wimbledon but smashed all of his rackets." That changed in 2001 when Ivanisevic won his first Wimbledon singles title. Ivanisevic breaks up to 60 rackets a year.

6. PANCHO GONZALES

Pancho Gonzales was one of the first tennis players to show anger on the court. The two-time U.S. Open champion vented his rage against opponents, officials, and spectators. It was said of Gonzales, "He's even tempered—he's always mad."

7. SIMONE MATHIEU

Simone Mathieu won the French Open women's singles titles in 1938 and 1939. The temperamental French star once had a linesman removed because she disagreed with a foot fault call against her. She sometimes slammed balls into the crowd, and on one occasion, nearly hit England's Queen Mary.

8. TIM HENMAN

Englishman Tim Henman was disqualified and fined $2,000 when he hit a ball in anger in a doubles match at Wimbledon in 1995. The ball struck a ball girl.

Henman expressed his sorrow and presented the girl with a bouquet of flowers.

q. **ALTHEA GIBSOn**

Althea Gibson let her anger get the best of her in the 1957 Victorian Championships in Melbourne, Australia. She slammed a ball into the crowd, barely missing the prime minister.

10. **MARCELO RIOS**

Each year at the French Open, the media presents a lemon prize for the player they determine to be the most unpleasant. In 2001, Marcelo Rios of Chile was awarded the dubious prize for the fifth time.

FANATICS

Sometimes tennis fans can become fanatics.

1. GUNTER PARCHE

The most shocking moment in tennis history took place at the women's tournament in Hamburg, Germany, in 1993. Nineteen-year-old Monica Seles, the world's number-one-ranked player, was playing a quarterfinal match against Magdalena Maleeva. During a change-over, Gunter Parche, a 38-year-old spectator, stabbed Seles below her left shoulder blade with a nine-inch knife. The reason for the attack was Parche's desire to see his favorite player, Steffi Graf, return to her number-one ranking. Seles did not play tournament tennis again for two years, and Graf did return to the top of the women's rankings.

2. **DUBRAVKO RAJCEVIC**

In April 2001, a jury in Miami, Florida, convicted Dubravko Rajcevic of stalking tennis star Martina Hingis. The 46-year-old naval architect contended that he did not want to hurt Hingis; he was trying to romance her. Rajcevic said he fell in love with Hingis while watching her play on television in 1999. Believing a relationship was possible, he began sending her love letters and traveled to Switzerland to deliver flowers to Hingis's home. The case took on an interesting twist when Hingis reportedly began dating the prosecuting attorney after the trial ended.

3. **INDIAN WELLS FANS**

Spectators were less than cordial to Venus and Serena Williams at the Indian Wells Tournament in California in March 2001. The fans were angered when Venus pulled out of a semifinal match with Serena because of a knee injury. Some fans were suspicious of the injury and believed the real reason for her withdrawal was that their father, Richard, instructed her to step aside so that Serena could rest before her final match against Kim Clijsters. According to Richard Williams, he and his daughters were subjected to racial taunts by some of the fans. One man reportedly said to Richard Williams, "I wish it was 1975, we'd skin you alive." Serena ignored the boos and won the championship match.

4. **LEW HOAD and FREW McMILLAN**

The men's doubles final at the 1972 Italian Open featured the team of Lew Hoad and Frew McMillan against
Ilie Nastase and Ion Tiriac. Hoad and McMillan trailed
3–6, 3–6, 6–4, 6–3, 5–3 when they asked for the lights
to be turned on. When their request was refused, they
defaulted. The crowd rioted, and the trophy presenta-
tion was moved inside to the stadium office to ensure
the players' safety.

5. **MAUREEN CONNOLLY**

Maureen Connolly won her first U.S. Open in 1951.
Following her victory, the 16-year-old signed autographs for her fans. She was tricked into signing a bad
check by a con man. Traumatized, Connolly never
signed autographs again after the incident.

6. **WIMBLEDON STREAKER**

The 1996 Wimbledon men's final matched Richard
Krajicek of the Netherlands against American Mali Vai
Washington. Before the match a blonde female streaker
ran across the court to the amusement of the players
and the fans. Krajicek regained his concentration and
won the match 6–3, 6–4, 6–3.

7. **MARY PIERCE**

In 2000, Mary Pierce became the first French woman
to win the French Open in 33 years. She became the

darling of the fans in Paris. The next year, however, the fickle fans hissed at Pierce when she lost 6–3, 6–3 to Anne Kremer of Luxembourg in her first match at the 2001 French Open.

8. HANA MANDLIKOVA

Martina Navratilova led Czechoslovakia to their first Federation Cup victory in 1975 and defected to the United States later that year. In 1986, she returned to Prague as a member of the American Federation Cup squad. Hana Mandlikova had led Czechoslovakia to three consecutive Federation Cup victories. Surprisingly, most of the Czech fans rooted for Navratilova in her match against Mandlikova. Inspired by the vocal support, Navratilova defeated Mandlikova 7–5, 6–1 and led the Americans to victory.

9. ANNA KOURNIKOVA FAN

At the 2001 Australian Open, a third-round women's doubles match featuring the team of Anna Kournikova and Barbara Schett was disrupted by a fan of Kournikova. A 15-year-old boy threw a smoking flare on the court, stopping action for 12 minutes.

10. 1969 DAVIS CUP FANS

The 1969 Davis Cup match between Great Britain and South Africa was held in Bristol, England. Demonstrators, protesting South Africa's policy of apartheid, hurled bags of flour onto the court.

Early Retirement

Tennis players usually begin their tournament careers as teenagers. Due to injury or a burnout, many are retired before they reach the age of 30.

1. MAUREEN CONNOLLY

Maureen Connolly was on top of the tennis world in 1954. The American teenager had won three consecutive U.S. Open and Wimbledon titles and was virtually unbeatable. Her reign as tennis's golden girl ended in the fall of 1954 when she was injured in a freak horse-riding accident. Colonel Merryboy, the horse she was riding, shied when an out-of-control cement lorry came around a corner. The horse fell onto Connolly's right leg, fracturing it and causing severe muscle damage. Unable to play competitive tennis, Connolly retired from the game at the age of 19.

2. **CHARLOTTE DOD**

Charlotte Dod was 15 when she won her first Wimbledon women's singles title in 1887. By the time Dod retired from tennis in 1893 at the age of 21, she was a five-time Wimbledon champion. She later became a champion golfer and archer.

3. **BJORN BORG**

Bjorn Borg had won six French Open and five Wimbledon men's singles titles by the time he was 24 years old. Having accomplished so much at such an early age, Borg lost motivation. He shocked the tennis world when he retired at age 27.

4. **DON BUDGE**

Don Budge was 23 when he became the first player to win tennis's Grand Slam in 1938. He retired from amateur tennis the next year. In 1941, the 26-year-old Budge retired from competitive tennis to begin a successful business career.

5. **TRACY AUSTIN**

Tracy Austin won two U.S. Open women's singles titles by age 18. She was in her early twenties when she retired from tournament tennis due to a series of nagging injuries to her elbow and neck. At age 26, she attempted a comeback in 1989, but it was aborted when she broke her leg in an automobile accident.

6. **DICK SEARS**

Dick Sears won seven consecutive U.S. Open men's singles titles from 1881 to 1887. Sears retired from tennis in 1887 at the age of 26.

7. **ANDREA JAEGER**

Andrea Jaeger began playing on the women's professional tour at 15. By the time she was 16, Jaeger was ranked in the top five. She was a finalist at the 1983 Wimbledon championships but would never win a Grand Slam singles title. A victim of burnout, Jaeger retired in her early twenties.

8. **GABRIELA SABATINI**

Gabriela Sabatini was a precocious talent, winning the world junior championships at 13. By age 18, Sabatini was the Olympic silver medalist. The Argentine was 20 when she won her first Grand Slam singles title at the 1990 U.S. Open. Sadly, it proved to be her last. A stomach injury forced Sabatini to retire in October 1996, at the age of 26.

9. **HANA MANDLIKOVA**

The 1978 world junior champion, Hana Mandlikova burst onto the tennis scene in 1980 with a victory in the Australian Open. She was still a teenager when she won the 1981 French Open. The highlight of her career was a memorable victory against Martina Navratilova in the women's singles final at the 1985 U.S. Open. Her final Grand Slam victory took place at the 1987 Australian Open. Mandlikova was still in her twenties when she retired from tennis.

10. **PANCHO SEGURA**

Pancho Segura of Ecuador won the U.S. indoor and clay court titles in the 1940s. He never won a Grand Slam singles title because he retired from amateur tennis at the age of 26 in 1947. Segura had a tremendously successful career as a professional and later as a tennis coach.

Incredible Injuries

A horseback riding injury may have cost Martina Hingis her chance to win tennis's Grand Slam in 1997. Hobbled, she lost in the finals of the French Open, her only Slam defeat that year. Each of these players had to overcome unusual injuries or illnesses.

1. JEAN-CLAUDE MOLINARI

Jean-Claude Molinari of France was one point away from an upset victory over Fred Stolle in a first-round match at the 1961 French Open. Molinari led 6–4, 7–5, 5–2, and was up 40–15 with a double match point when he tore his Achilles tendon and had to withdraw.

2. MAY BUNDY

At the 1930 U.S. Open, May Bundy fractured her leg in a match. The plucky player insisted on finishing the match while using a crutch.

3. FRANK SHIELDS

Frank Shields fell and injured his leg in a semifinal match against Jean Borotra at Wimbledon in 1931. He managed to win the match but had to forfeit the championship match against Sidney Wood.

4. CHRISTINE TRUMAN

In the 1961 women's championship match at Wimbledon, Christine Truman led Angela Mortimer 6–4, 4–3 when she slipped on the grass and fell heavily. Truman injured her right thigh but was able to continue. Slowed by the leg injury, Truman lost 4–6, 6–4, 7–5.

5. BILL TILDEN

In 1922, Bill Tilden pricked the middle finger on his right hand on a wire backstop during an exhibition in Bridgeton, New Jersey. The wound became infected, and the tip of his finger had to be amputated after gangrene set in. The handicap did not affect his play, and Tilden won four more U.S. Open championships.

6. GOTTFRIED VON CRAMM

Gottfried von Cramm lost part of his index finger as a child when he was bitten while feeding sugar to a horse. The German became one of the best tennis players in the world and was the French Open men's champion in 1934 and 1936.

7. **WIMBLEDON THROAT**

The 1934 Wimbledon championships was disrupted by a mysterious throat illness that affected 63 players. The throat infection had symptoms similar to diphtheria and left the players unable to speak. The mysterious illness was referred to as "Wimbledon throat."

8. **MARY PIERCE**

In April 2001, Mary Pierce strained her back while throwing a medicine ball during an exercise routine. Due to the injury, she was unable to play in the Bausch and Lomb Championships in Florida.

9. **YEVGENY KAFELNIKOV**

Russian Yevgeny Kafelnikov won the 1996 French Open. Just prior to the 1997 Australian Open, Kafelnikov broke his hand hitting a punching bag. He was forced to withdraw from the tournament.

10. **BRIE RIPPNER**

In 1999, the Australian Open was moved to a new tennis complex at Melbourne Park. The first match in the new Vodafone Arena matched Monica Seles and Brie Rippner. In the second game of the first set, Rippner fell on the sticky new surface and was unable to continue. The match lasted less than five minutes.

It's a good thing Yevgeny Kafelnikov picked tennis instead of boxing. A year after winning the 1996 French Open, his first Grand Slam title, the Russian had to withdraw from the 1997 Australian Open after breaking his hand hitting a punching bag. Kafelnikov would return to Australia and take home the championship in 1999.

Match Points

We conclude with notable tennis lasts.

1. JOSHUA PIM

Joshua Pim was the last Wimbledon champion to play under an assumed name. Joshua Pim, a physician from Ireland, won Wimbledon in 1893 and 1894. Pim played under an alias because he was afraid that his status as a tennis champion might adversely affect his medical practice.

2. FRANK RIESLEY and SYDNEY SMITH

The last match at Wimbledon decided by a coin toss occurred in 1904. Frank Riesley and Sydney Smith were tied at two sets apiece in their semifinal match when they decided to flip a coin rather than play a fifth set. The two men, friends and doubles partners, believed that if they conserved energy, the winner of the coin toss would have a better chance of winning the final. Riesley won the coin toss but lost the championship match to Laurie Doherty 6–1, 7–5, 8–6. Riesley and Smith also lost the men's doubles match to Reggie and Laurie Doherty 6–1, 6–2, 6–4.

3. BEVERLY FLEITZ

The last tennis player to withdraw from Wimbledon because she was pregnant was Beverly Fleitz. A finalist at Wimbledon in 1955, she was the second seed in 1956. Although she won the first three matches, Fleitz did not feel well. An examination revealed that she was pregnant. Rather than risk injury to her baby, she withdrew from the tournament.

4. M. H. DE AMORIN

The last player at Wimbledon to serve 17 consecutive double faults was M. H. de Amorin of Brazil at Wimbledon in 1957. Nervous in her first Wimbledon match, she lost to L. B. Thung of Holland 6–3, 4–6, 6–1.

5. FRED PERRY

The last Englishman to win the men's singles title at Wimbledon was Fred Perry. He won his third and final Wimbledon championship in 1936.

6. CHALLENGE ROUND

The last challenge round at Wimbledon was played in 1921. In those days the previous year's winner did not have to play until the championship match while everyone else competed for the chance to play in the final. Bill Tilden, the 1920 champion, retained his title with a five-set win against B. I. Norton.

7. **MANUELA MALEEVA**

Rain delays forced Maleeva to play her quarterfinal, semifinal, and final matches on May 28, 1984. In her quarterfinal match she defeated Virginia Ruzici 7–6, 4–6, 6–2. Maleeva defeated Carling Bassett Seguso 6–2, 6–2 in the semifinal. She capped off her day with an impressive 6–3, 6–3 victory over Chris Evert in the final.

8. **YVON PETRA**

Yvon Petra was the last men's player to wear long flannel trousers while winning at Wimbledon. In 1946, he defeated Geoff Brown 6–2, 6–4, 7–9, 5–7, 6–4 to win the men's singles title. Future champions wore white shorts.

9. **JOHN McENROE**

The last player to win Wimbledon using a wooden racket was John McEnroe. He won his first Wimbledon title with a wooden racket in 1981. McEnroe won Wimbledon in 1983 and 1984 with a metal racket.

10. **JOHN NEWCOMBE**

The last amateur player to win Wimbledon was John Newcombe in 1967. The next year, professionals were permitted to compete. Newcombe won Wimbledon in 1970 and 1971 as a professional.

Bibliography

Brown, Gerry, and Michael Morrison. *2001 ESPN Sports Almanac.* New York: Hyperion, 2000.

Clark, Patrick. *Sports Firsts.* New York: Facts on File, 1981.

Clerici, Gianni. *The Ultimate Tennis Book.* Chicago: Follett Publishing, 1975.

Collins, Bud, and Zander Hollander. *Bud Collins' Modern Encyclopedia of Tennis.* Detroit, Mich.: Visible Ink, 1994.

Evans, Richard. *McEnroe, Taming the Talent.* New York: Stephen Greene Press, 1990.

Fischler, Stan, and Shirley Fischler. *The Best, Worst, and Most Unusual in Sports.* New York: Fawcett Crest, 1977.

Gillmeister, Heiner. *Tennis: A Cultural History.* London: Leicester University Press, 1997.

King, Billie Jean, and Cynthia Starr. *We Have Come A Long Way.* New York: McGraw-Hill, 1988.

Minton, Robert. *Forest Hills.* Philadelphia: J. P. Lippincott Co., 1975.

Parsons, John. *The Ultimate Encyclopedia of Tennis.* London: Carlton Books, 1998.

Phillips, Louis, and Burnham Holmes. *The Complete Book of Sports Nicknames.* Los Angeles: Renaissance Books, 1998.

Shannon, Bill. *Official Encyclopedia of Tennis.* New York: Harper & Row, 1979.

Snyder, John. *Tennis.* San Francisco: Chronicle Books, 1993.

Tingay, Lance. *Guinness Book of Tennis Facts & Feats.* London: Guinness Books, 1983.

Tinling, Ted, and Rod Humphries. *Love and Faults.* New York: Crown, 1979.

Wallechinsky, David. *The Complete Book of the Summer Olympics.* Woodstock: Overlook Press, 2000.

Index

Agassi, Andre, 36, 63, 70, 111, 117, 141, 194, 201, 202, 203, 226, 229

Agassi, Mike, 194

Allen, Leslie, 221

Allison, Wilmer, 144

Amritraj, Vijay, 36

Andrew, Jorge, 145

Arias, Jimmy, 70, 74

Arresse, Jordi, 148

Arth, Jeanne, 67

Ashe, Arthur, 26, 27, 33, 78, 131, 132, 152, 172, 198, 217, 223, 231

Aussem, Cissy, 185

Austin, Bunny, 19, 58, 84, 243

Austin, John, 189

Austin, Pam, 190

Austin, Tracy, 73, 90, 116, 141, 175, 189, 266

Babcock, Carolin, 87

Badderley, Herbert, 135, 189

Badderley, Wilfred, 135, 189

Baker, Beverly, 21

Barrett, Herbert, 244

Bartkowicz, Peaches, 44, 57, 216

Becker, Boris, 17, 19, 69, 111, 140, 141, 148, 160, 169, 171, 205, 233, 256

Berbarian, Yulia, 188

Betz, Pauline, 215

Bingley, Blanche, 78, 134

Blair, Roseleena, 252

Boland, John Pius, 149

Bolton, Nancy Wynne, 67

Boothby, Dora, 181

Borg, Bjorn, 26, 28, 43, 67, 70, 84, 110, 118, 126, 138, 139, 141, 161, 163, 184, 223, 228,

Borg, Bjorn (continued)
229, 232, 255, 266

Borotra, Jean, 48, 77, 103, 184, 246, 270

Bowrey, Bill, 81

Bricka, Justina, 86

Bromwich, John, 19, 66, 83, 102

Brookes, Norman, 135, 244

Broquedis, Marguerite, 48

Brough, Louise, 83, 86, 91, 106, 126, 169

Brown, Bill, 81

Brown, Geoff, 275

Brown, Mary, 59

Brown, Nick, 235

Brown, Tom, 86

Browne, Mary, 4, 179, 211, 253

Brugnon, Jacques, 48, 246

Budge, Don, 3, 58, 119, 231, 266

Bueno, Maria, 67, 124, 129, 164, 169

Bundy, May, 269

Bunge, Bettina, 23

Capriati, Jennifer, 75, 234, 252

Caroline, Princess, 205

Casals, Rosemary, 40, 44, 66, 131, 155, 165, 207, 216

Casey, Miss, 214

Cash, Pat, 160, 173

Cavis-Brown, Dorothy, 242

Chambers, Dorothea, 134, 181, 232

Chang, Michael, 19, 22, 70, 140, 148, 164, 172, 258

Chymreva, Natasha, 76

Clijsters, Kim, 262

Cochell, Earl, 256

Cochet, Henri, 48, 117, 129, 168, 184

Coen, Wilbur, 145, 243

Connolly, Maureen, 3, 38, 61, 74, 99, 123, 180, 227, 263, 265

Connors, Jimmy, 15, 28, 29, 62, 79, 91, 95, 109, 117, 118, 119, 138, 141, 160, 163, 168, 171, 172, 179, 198, 201, 204, 209, 224, 231, 232, 245, 252

Cooper, Ashley, 238

Cooper, Charlotte, 135, 194

Cornejo, Pat, 145

Courier, Jim, 79, 148, 162, 164, 248

Court, Margaret Smith, 45, 57, 65, 91, 97, 105, 107, 114, 122, 126, 138, 139, 156, 164, 165, 169, 176, 208, 211, 224, 230, 238

Cox, Mark, 86

Crawford, Jack, 248

Crookenden, Ian, 242

Crosby, Cathy Lee, 35

Curren, Kevin, 19, 199, 233

Dalton, Judy, 44, 216

D'Alvarez, Lili, 215

Davenport, Lindsay, 192, 219

Davis, Dwight, 143

De Amorin, M. H., 274

Decugis, Marie, 149

Decugis, Max, 147, 149, 209

Dell, Dick, 82, 85

Dementieva, Elena, 150

De Stefani, Giorgio, 14, 144

Dibbs, Eddie, 47, 157

Dibley, Colin, 17

Dod, Charlotte, 21, 39, 49, 73, 121, 209, 266

Doherty, Laurence, 150, 187, 274

Doherty, Reggie, 150, 187, 274

Dokic, Damir, 191

Dokic, Jelena, 191

Donnisthorpe, F. W., 14

Drobny, Jaroslav, 32, 62, 83, 159, 169

Duggan, Will, 244

Du Pont, Margaret Osborne, 78, 83, 86, 91, 106, 126

Dwight, James, 8

Edberg, Stefan, 140, 141, 148, 164, 172, 239, 241

Edmondson, Mark, 190

Emerson, Roy, 93, 101, 103, 105, 118, 127, 160, 184, 186, 223, 235

Ermakova, Angela, 205

Evert, Chris, 54, 73, 75, 90, 98, 113, 114, 123, 125, 138, 139, 141, 155, 158, 160, 164, 175, 176, 177, 195, 201, 204, 223, 235, 237, 275

Evert, Jimmy, 195

Fageros, Karol, 40

Falkenburg, Robert, 19, 85, 86

Fernandez, Gigi, 22, 65, 154

Fernandez, Mary Joe, 22, 65, 74, 154, 156

Fick, Sigrid, 148

Fields, W. C., 37

Fillol, Jaime, 145

Flam, Herbie, 22, 63

Fleitz, Beverly, 274

Fleming, Peter, 65

Fletcher, Ken, 65, 211

Forbes, Gordon, 86

Forget, Guy, 61, 153, 190

Fraser, Neale, 61, 78, 79, 102, 170

Frawley, John, 87
Fritz, Harry, 145
Fromholtz, Dianne, 190
Fry, Shirley, 180, 181

Gable, Clark, 37, 38
Gannon, Joy, 42
Gardini, Fausto, 55, 245
Garrison, Zina, 218, 220
Gasiorek, Wieslaw, 82
Gerulaitis, Vitas, 45, 164, 173, 210, 232
Gibson, Althea, 31, 67, 217, 260
Glyn, William, 2
Godfree, Kitty, 44, 149, 211
Godfree, Leslie, 211
Gomez, Andres, 63
Gonzales, Pancho, 17, 77, 82, 85, 117, 161, 223, 259
Goolagong, Evonne, 45, 98, 114, 130, 141, 156, 163, 223
Gore, Arthur, 77, 244
Gore, Spencer, 1
Gottfried, Brian, 66, 144, 156, 243
Graebner, Carole, 85
Graebner, Clark, 242, 257
Graf, Peter, 194
Graf, Steffi, 73, 75, 97, 107, 114, 115, 122, 138, 139, 141, 161, 175, 181, 185, 194, 201, 203, 220, 226, 239, 261
Grant, Bitsy, 58
Guernsey, Frank, 87
Gunnarson, Jan, 87

Hadow, Frank, 25
Hagey, Cari, 241
Haillet, Robert, 185
Hamilton, Willoughby, 53
Hanks, Carol, 86
Hansell, Ellen, 21, 213
Hard, Darlene, 67
Hart, Doris, 106, 180, 181, 227
Hartley, John, 27, 182, 241
Hawton, Mary, 67
Hearst, William Randolph, 37
Heathcote, J. M., 14
Heldman, Gladys, 44, 215
Heldman, Julie, 43, 216
Henman, Tim, 259
Henry V, 6
Henry VIII, 6
Hepner, Jean, 90
Hewitt, Bob, 103, 152
Hewitt, Lleyton, 71
Hickey, William, 7
Higueras, Jose, 183
Hillyard, George, 150

Hingis, Martina, 74, 141, 151, 176, 191, 192, 234, 253, 262, 269

Hoad, Lew, 20, 79, 117, 159, 165, 238, 263

Hoepner, Bill, 244

Holcroft-Watson, Mrs., 185

Holmburg, Ron, 86

Holmes, Tully, 220

Hopman, Harry, 48

Horvath, Kathy, 28

Huiskamp, Miss, 179

Hutton, Barbara, 204

Ivanisevic, Goran, 18, 61, 137, 159, 235, 258

Jacobs, Helen, 87, 225

Jaeger, Andrea, 74, 177, 267

Jarryd, Anders, 67

Jedzejowska, Jedwiga, 225

Johnston, Bill, 126, 225

Jones, Ann, 62, 176, 189

Jones, Arnold, 209

Jordan, Kathy, 91

Kafelnikov, Yevgeny, 271, 272

Kapp, Ron, 244

Kavanaugh, Collette, 241

Kessler, Guus, 147

King, Billie Jean, 44, 45, 46, 62, 66, 98, 106, 114, 124, 131, 138, 156, 161, 164, 165, 175, 207, 215, 216, 224, 230, 235, 238, 247

Kinsey, Howard, 4, 89, 211

Kodes, Jan, 250

Korda, Petr, 61

Koring, Dora, 148

Kournikova, Anna, 40, 201, 250, 251, 264

Kovacs, Frank, 245

Kramer, Jack, 17, 117, 186, 223

Krajicek, Richard, 263

Kremer, Anne, 264

Krickstein, Aaron, 69

Kuerten, Gustavo, 139

Lacoste, Rene, 40, 48, 117, 168, 231

Larned, Bill, 79, 134

Larsen, Art, 63, 248

Laver, Rod, 27, 48, 61, 82, 94, 102, 111, 117, 118, 125, 165, 172, 184, 223, 224, 230

Leach, Dick, 85

Leconte, Henri, 61, 131

Lendl, Ivan, 22, 33, 45, 95, 109, 119, 127, 138, 141, 160, 168, 171, 183

Lenglen, Charles, 193

Lenglen, Suzanne, 3, 4, 25, 41, 98, 107, 121, 127, 130, 138, 139, 161, 179, 180, 193, 209, 227, 229, 232, 246, 253

Lewis, Chris, 234

Lloyd, David, 257

Lloyd, John, 204

Long, Thelma Coyne, 67

Louie, Peanut, 57

Louis X, 5

Lowe, Gordon, 147

Lutz, Bob, 165

Majoli, Iva, 234

Maleeva, Katerina, 188

Maleeva, Magdalena, 188, 261

Maleeva, Manuela, 188, 275

Mallory, Molla, 3, 25, 79, 99, 126, 133, 179

Mandlikova, Hana, 130, 160, 176, 218, 264, 267

Marble, Alice, 37, 87, 181

Margot, Lady, 213

Marshall, William, 1

Martin, Todd, 157

Martinez, Conchita, 116, 176

Masters, Geoff, 243

Mathieu, Simone, 259

Mauresmo, Amelie, 253

Mayer, Gene, 190

Mayer, Sandy, 190

McEnroe, John, 15, 45, 46, 51, 52, 62, 65, 83, 110, 118, 119, 126, 141, 163, 164, 168, 183, 197, 202, 204, 210, 223, 224, 228, 229, 232, 234, 245, 255, 257, 275

McGregor, Ken, 33, 68

McGuire, Patti, 204

McKane, Kathleen, 28, 180

McKinley, Chuck, 160

McMillan, Frew, 263

McNeil, Lori, 220

McNeill, Don, 87

Mecir, Miroslav, 49

Melville, Kerry, 44, 216

Merlo, Beppino, 23, 246

Molinari, Jean-Claude, 269

Moran, Gussy, 39, 40, 83, 86, 215, 247

Morozova, Olga, 235

Mortensen, Michael, 87

Mortimer, Angela, 270

Mottram, Buster, 144

Mozur, Tom, 85

Mronz, Alexander, 258

Mulloy, Gardnar, 79, 87, 243, 256

Muster, Thomas, 61, 148

Nastase, Ilie, 26, 34, 51, 111, 131, 141, 161, 245, 248, 257, 263

Navratilova, Martina, 28, 44, 61, 90, 91, 92, 98, 105, 113, 114, 116, 122, 125, 137, 138, 141, 151, 158, 160, 176, 177, 193, 209, 220, 223, 237, 250, 252, 264, 267

Nelson, Judy, 252

Nelson, Ricky, 36

Nelson, Vicky, 90

Newcombe, John, 63, 101, 117, 118, 159, 168, 235, 243, 275

Nielsen, Kurt, 233

Noah, Yannick, 152

Norton, B. I., 275

Novotna, Jana, 22, 176, 185

Nuthall, Betty, 59, 194

Nuthall, Stuart, 194

Okker, Tom, 27, 33, 48, 65, 156

Olmedo, Alex, 86, 153, 199

O'Neal, Tatum, 202

Orantes, Manuel, 63, 129, 184

Osuna, Rafael, 129, 198

Outerbridge, Mary, 7

Palfrey, Sarah, 53, 87, 215

Panatta, Adriano, 43, 183

Parche, Gunter, 261

Parke, James, 150

Parker, Frank, 78, 185

Pasarell, Charlie, 82, 86

Pascual, Virginia, 234

Patty, Budge, 58, 79, 83, 185

Pecci, Victor, 87

Peret, Paul, 4

Pernfors, Mikael, 256

Perry, Fred, 3, 35, 94, 117, 179, 248, 274

Petra, Yvon, 153, 275

Phillips-Moore, Barry, 15

Pickard, Tony, 242

Pierce, Jim, 193

Pierce, Mary, 152, 193, 262, 271

Pietrangeli, Nicola, 145

Pigeon, Kristy, 44, 216

Pilic, Nikki, 86, 249

Pim, Joshua, 273

Pioline, Cedric, 157

Pohmann, Hans-Joachim, 257

Pyle, C. C., 4

Quist, Adrian, 66

Rafter, Patrick, 117, 159, 172, 173, 205

Rahim, Haroon, 144

Rajcevic, Dubravko, 262

Ralston, Dennis, 148

Ramirez, Raul, 66, 243

Rebeuh, Bruno, 258

Redl, Hans, 9, 144

Rees-Lewis, Jacqueline, 35

Renshaw, Ernest, 133, 188, 209

Renshaw, Willie, 95, 117, 125, 133, 182, 188

Richards, Renee, 210

Richards, Vincent, 69

Richey, Cliff, 86, 189, 245

Richey, Nancy, 44, 85, 164, 189, 216

Riesley, Frank, 273

Riessen, Marty, 33

Riggs, Bobby, 27, 38, 45, 54, 207, 208, 216, 247

Rinaldi, Kathy, 73

Rinkel, Jean, 180

Rios, Marcelo, 260

Rippner, Brie, 271

Ritchie, Josiah, 150

Robbins, F.D., 82

Roche, Tony, 62, 82, 165, 172

Roddick, Andy, 19, 71

Roosevelt, Ellen, 188

Roosevelt, Grace, 188

Rose, Mervyn, 238

Rosewall, Ken, 28, 32, 53, 62, 78, 95, 103, 118, 120, 159, 165, 171, 179, 224, 230, 231, 233, 237

Rosset, Marc, 148

Rubin, Chandra, 220

Rusedski, Greg, 18, 153

Ruzici, Virginia, 275

Ryan, Elizabeth, 49, 90, 107, 161, 227, 253

Sabatini, Gabriela, 131, 141, 176, 267

Sampras, Pete, 43, 70, 93, 110, 117, 118, 138, 140, 141, 148, 153, 157, 159, 164, 166, 167, 172, 173, 226, 229

Sampson, Julie, 180

Sangster, Michael, 18

Savitt, Dick, 17, 42

Scaino, Antonio, 13

Schett, Barbara, 264

Schloss, Len, 85

Schmidt, Ulf, 243

Schomburgk, Heinrich, 148

Scott, Gene, 86

Schroeder, Ted, 85

Sears, Richard, 2, 134, 267

Sedgman, Frank, 33, 68, 102, 117, 169

Segal, Abe, 86, 242

Segura, Pancho, 86, 197, 268

Seguso, Carling Bassett, 275

Seixas, Vic, 81, 233

Seles, Monica, 53, 61, 75, 99, 114, 116, 124, 141, 220, 226, 239, 261, 271

Setterwall, Gunnar, 148

Shields, Brooke, 35, 202, 203

Shields, Frank, 26, 35, 202, 270

Shriver, Pam, 41, 75, 90, 92, 125, 155, 177, 218

Slowe, Lucy, 220

Smashnova, Anna, 58

Smid, Tomas, 256

Smith, Sydney, 273

Smith, Stan, 47, 145, 161, 165, 199

Smylie, Elizabeth, 91

Smyth, Patty, 204

Snodgrass, Harvey, 4

Solomon, Harold, 47

Sperling, Hilda, 181

Stammers, Kay, 87

Stewart, Hugh, 85

Stewart, Pat, 40

Stich, Michael, 141, 148, 173, 241

St. Leger Gould, V., 241

Stolle, Fred, 103, 160, 186, 223, 235, 269

Stove, Betty, 157

Stuart, Betty Ann, 210

Stuyvesant, Peter, 6

Sukova, Helena, 22, 91, 158, 195

Sukova, Vera, 195, 235

Susman, Karen, 235, 238

Sutter, Chris, 84

Sutton, May, 2

Talbert, Bill, 86, 87

Tanner, Roscoe, 18

Tapscott, Ruth, 214

Tarango, Jeff, 258

Taylor, Roger, 82, 258

Tennant, Eleanor, 38, 227

Thung, L. B., 274

Tilden, Bill, 17, 38, 94, 102, 117, 118, 126, 134, 138, 167, 184, 209, 225, 231, 249, 270, 275

Tinling, Ted, 39, 40, 41, 42

Tiriac, Ion, 34, 248, 263

Todd, Pat, 83

Townsend, Bertha, 59

Trabert, Tony, 32, 198, 233, 237

Traun, Fritz, 149

Truman, Christine, 270

Turnbull, Oswald, 32

Turnbull, Wendy, 49, 204

Turner, Lesley, 238

Tyrwhitt-Drake, A., 23

Ulrich, Torben, 86, 244

Van Alen, Jimmy, 12

Van Bay, Von, 145

Vance, Miss, 214

Van Dillen, Erik, 145

Van Patten, Vince, 36

Van Ryn, Marjorie, 87

Vicario, Arantxa Sanchez, 47, 160, 175, 220

Vilas, Guillermo, 61, 110, 161, 172, 205

Vines, Ellsworth, 19, 22, 32, 58, 84

Vlasto, Diddie, 253

Von Cramm, Gottfried, 179, 204, 231, 270

Wade, Virginia, 46, 116, 157, 175, 238

Washington, Mali Vai, 263

Watson, Lilian, 2

Watson, Maud, 2, 14, 44, 213

White, Anne, 41

Wightman, Hazel, 179, 214

Wilander, Mats, 70, 83, 239

Wilding, Tony, 135, 244

Wilkison, Tim, 47

Williams, Richard (*Titanic* survivor), 242

Williams, Richard (father of Serena and Venus), 192, 262

Williams, Serena, 150, 188, 192, 210, 218, 219, 262

Williams, Venus, 42, 43, 121, 139, 150, 188, 192, 210, 218, 219, 262

Williams, Vincent, 4

Wills, Helen, 28, 54, 89, 98, 106, 123, 138, 161, 225, 229

Wilson, Robert, 86

Wingfield, Walter, 7, 10, 14

Wood, Sidney, 26, 270

Woodforde, Mark, 65

Woodridge, Todd, 65

Woosnam, Max, 32

Zerlentis, Anasthasios, 147

Ziegenfuss, Val, 44, 216

Zvereva, Natasha, 68, 181

About the Author

Floyd Conner is the author of more than a dozen books. His sports books include *Basketball's Most Wanted, Golf's Most Wanted, Baseball's Most Wanted, Day by Day in Cincinnati Bengals History,* and *This Date in Sports History.* He also coauthored *Day by Day in Cincinnati Reds History* and the best-selling *365 Sports Facts a Year Calendar.* He lives in Cincinnati with his wife, Susan, and son, Travis.